INSIGHTISM

To Treat Congenital & Behavioural Disorders of State

Sarvar Allam

Notion Press Media Pvt Ltd

No. 50, Chettiyar Agaram Main Road,
Vanagaram, Chennai, Tamil Nadu – 600 095

First Published by Notion Press 2021
Copyright © Sarvar Allam 2021
All Rights Reserved.

ISBN 978-1-63886-510-0

To

Bill Gates

&

**All Youth Activists who strive to make
the world a better place to live in**

CONTENTS

PREFACE

This book in new genre of 'popular political science' attempts to expose the critical deficiencies of modern state system that are creating hurdles in addressing apocalyptic global risks and reaching UN's Sustainable Development Goals. It introduces a new **Unified Political Theory**, prioritising the political objects that are commonly applicable at state as well as global level with the basic intention of ensuring a peaceful, harmonious and sustainable global society and for maintaining the present momentum in the progress of human civilization. The proposed concept of **INSIGHTISM** attempts to remedy the shortcomings of the modern state system enabling unhindered delivery of **Universal Common Good** to all. Though this book is not meant for academics and research scholars, its fresh perspective on the nearly 400 years old state system and effort to pitch for a homogeneous and inclusive political theory in response to the present deteriorating political and economic conditions of the world would definitely kindle the interest of students of political science and development economics, prompting them to make further studies in this direction and develop new ideas and find innovative solutions. More importantly, this book would serve as a reference guide and a motivating tool for the young activists already involved in the betterment of human life and society.

Disclaimer: I am not a scholar in political science or development economics.

– Sarvar Allam

26th Apr 2021

1

INTRODUCTION

YOUTH – POTENTIAL SAVIOUR OF THE WORLD

"We live in an age when to be young and to be indifferent can be no longer synonymous. We must prepare for the coming hour. The claims of the future are represented by suffering millions; and the Youth of a Nation are the trustees of Posterity."

– Benjamin Disraeli (1804–1881)

In September, 2018, Ffion Hâf Jones, a 13-year-old student from Ysgol Llanhari, Rhondda Cynon Taf wrote to Welsh Youth Parliament,

"We, young people, are the future of our community and the future of our country. It is therefore very important that we can express our views on decisions that will certainly affect the future in which we will be a part."

Statesman and two-time Prime Minister of Britain, Benjamin Disraeli of 19th century and a totally unfamiliar teenager Ffion Hâf Jones of 21st century have identical view on the ability of the youth in shaping the future. But there is no point in carrying on this hope for centuries together, simply witnessing millions and millions of people to undergo sufferings from persistent hunger, poverty, malnutrition, illiteracy, preventable diseases, violence, natural disasters, and forced displacement, alongside the degradation of the planet Earth to a dangerously inhabitable condition for the present as well as future generations. In a world where climate change wreaks havoc on our economies, societies and environment, where unemployment and inequalities are rampant and where trust in international cooperation is falling, what can keep us from losing faith that the world 2030 will be a better place for everyone? UN Department of Economic and Social Affairs'(DESA) World Youth Report offers one good reason for optimism: THE NEXT GENERATION IS DIFFERENT. Young people are more optimistic about the future than older generations. Despite facing much higher unemployment rates, more instability and lower wages than their predecessors, today's youth are entering adulthood confidently knowing well that they can build a better future for themselves and for the generations to come. Noble laureate Kailash Satyarthi says, "The power of youth is the common wealth for the entire world. The faces of young people are the faces of our past, our present and our future. No segment in the society can match with the power, idealism, enthusiasm and courage of the young people."

Youth population is at its peak today and at the same time the rising scale of challenges they are facing now is unprecedented in the history of the world. But the youth are undeterred and ready to meet the challenges boldly with positive mindset. Number of women and young girls now taking part in social and community development activities is more than ever in human history. Previous generations have never seen Malalas and Gretas articulating critical social issues, attracting international attention. Youth comprehend problems quickly and know how to use the latest technology aptly to address them. They are outgoing and willing to travel and work in any community, crossing all societal and geographical barriers. With their unassuming attitude and eloquence, they can convince everyone with their point of view and generate momentum naturally among the people they are working for. The youth also know the urgency of mitigating the present catastrophic global risks and thereby saving the livelihood of their own and future generations. Young people are the potential saviour of this world to ensure a peaceful, harmonious and sustainable world for all, and they only can do this.

GLOBAL RISKS

This planet Earth with its natural resources and atmosphere, and the solar system are common for all people living in this world, who hail from the same lineage of homo sapiens claimed to have existed some 200,000 years ago in Africa. Still, the dividends of such common natural resources are denied to billions of people only because of their country/race/community/family of birth. It is said that human as a species is in the process of evolving into super-human with extraordinary power and intelligence naturally as well as customized by genetic technology. The progress made in medical science has considerably increased the average life span of humans and our exploration of universe has progressed from Moon to Mars in recent times. But the mankind has miserably failed in the simple task of ensuring bare minimum living conditions, wherein all people of the world can live with basic needs of life and progress according to their capabilities. This paradoxical coexistence of remarkable achievements of mankind alongside the miserable failures of our generation is analogous to a painter who has adorned his house with fabulous paintings; but failed to paint the patchy and peeling walls on which the paintings are hanging.

In Global Shapers Survey 2017 conducted by the World Economic Forum, millennials (persons aging between 18 and 35 years old) have identified the following 10 issues as most challenging to the world: -

10. Lack of economic opportunity and employment (12.1%)

9. Safety/security/wellbeing (14.1%)

8. Lack of education (15.9%)

7. Food and water security (18.2%)

6. Government accountability and transparency/corruption (22.7%)

5. Religious conflicts (23.9%)

4. Poverty (29.2%)

3. Inequality (income, discrimination) (30.8%)

2. Large scale conflict/wars (38.9%)

1. Climate change/destruction of nature (48.8%)

Among the above most challenging global risks, climate change, poverty, inequality and large scale and religious armed conflicts can be considered as primary risks and other risks as secondary. Because, the primary risks are intertwined with each other that engender other risks. Progress made in the mitigation of the primary risks will naturally address the problems of secondary risks too. Any slight moderation made in the primary risks is likely to trigger positive chain reaction in the matrix of human development. The above global risks are also covered in the following 17 Sustainable Development Goals (SDGs) to be achieved by the year 2030, identified and planned by the United Nations (UN) in 2015 as a "blueprint to achieve a better and more sustainable future for all".

GOAL 1: No Poverty

GOAL 2: Zero Hunger

GOAL 3: Good Health and Well-being

GOAL 4: Quality Education

GOAL 5: Gender Equality

GOAL 6: Clean Water and Sanitation

GOAL 7: Affordable and Clean Energy

GOAL 8: Decent Work and Economic Growth

GOAL 9: Industry, Innovation and Infrastructure

GOAL 10: Reduced Inequalities

GOAL 11: Sustainable Cities and Communities

GOAL 12: Responsible Consumption and Production

GOAL 13: Climate Action

GOAL 14: Life Below Water

GOAL 15: Life on Land

GOAL 16: Peace Justice and Strong Institutions

GOAL 17: Partnerships for the Goals

All the above 17 SDGs are easily achievable, if the above identified primary global risks are mitigated concurrently.

Among the many inequalities hampering human development, economic inequality is the crucial one. Poverty lies at one end of the spectrum of the economic inequality, and as per recent studies, inequality and climate change are strongly connected. After the drop in the incidence of wars between nations after World War II, most of the intra-state armed conflicts occur now due to delicate socio-economic conditions and religious and sectarian rivalries. In some cases, state itself unleashes violence on its citizens. These critical risk factors have already made many states fragile and conflict affected. On the other side, rising trend of national populism in developed and developing nations hinders the existing channels of aid and income to the downtrodden communities of less developed countries. The populists are also sceptical about the dangerous consequences of climate change. The current break-down of world economy due to coronavirus pandemic with its conceivable long-term effect has further complicated the solution to the above problems. If these prioritized global risks are not addressed immediately, the present COVID-19 pandemic driven economic crisis is likely to combine the frequencies of all these risks, leading to a major breakdown of the existing fragile equilibrium of social, political and economic order of the world and reverse the overall progress made in human development in the past few decades.

Climate Change

After realizing the scientific evidence of global warming and its catastrophic effects not only on the human beings, but also on all the creatures and plants surviving on land and under water, climate change is placed at the top in every list of global challenges/threats/risks that endanger the world. Climate Change is a defining issue of our time and we are at a defining moment. From shifting weather patterns that threaten food production, to rising sea levels that increase the risk of disastrous flooding, the impacts of climate change are global in scope and unprecedented in scale. Without taking drastic climate positive action today, adapting to these impacts in the future will be more difficult and costly. After more than a century and a half of industrialization, deforestation, and increasing transportation, quantities of greenhouse gases (GHGs), i.e., Carbon Dioxide, Methane, Nitrous Oxide and Fluorinated Gases in the atmosphere have risen to unprecedented record levels. Greenhouse gases trap heat and make the planet warmer. Human activities such as transportation, production of electricity, agriculture, industrial and other activities in which fossil fuels are burnt are mostly responsible for the increase in greenhouse gases in the atmosphere over the past 150 years.

As populations, economies and standards of living grow, so does the cumulative level of greenhouse gas emissions. The concentration of GHGs in the earth's atmosphere is directly linked to the average global temperature on Earth. Carbon dioxide (CO_2) which constitutes two-thirds of total GHGs is largely a product of burning fossil fuels. Given current concentrations and ongoing emissions of greenhouse gases, it is likely that by the end of this century global mean temperature will continue to rise above the pre-industrial level. The world's oceans will warm and ice melt will continue. Average sea level rise is predicted to be 24–30 cm by 2065 and 40–63 cm by 2100 relative to the reference period of 1986–2005. The looming danger is that many aspects of climate change will persist for centuries, even if GHGs emissions are stopped.

There are alarming evidences that important tipping points, leading to irreversible changes in major ecosystems and the planetary climate system, may already have been reached or passed. Ecosystems as diverse as the Amazon rainforest and the Arctic tundra, may be approaching thresholds of dramatic change through warming and drying. Mountain glaciers are in alarming retreat and the downstream effects of reduced water supply in the driest months will have repercussions that transcend generations. Limiting global warming to 1.5°C would require "rapid and far-reaching" transitions in land, energy, industry, buildings, transport, and cities. Global net human-caused emissions of carbon dioxide (CO_2) would need to fall by about 45 percent from 2010 levels by 2030, reaching 'net zero' around 2050. This means that any remaining emissions would need to be balanced by removing CO2 from the air. [1]

Affirming the fallout of climate change, NASA reports that global climate change has already had observable effects on the environment. Glaciers have shrunk, ice on rivers and lakes is breaking up earlier, plant and animal ranges have shifted and trees are flowering sooner. Effects that scientists had predicted in the past would result from global climate change are now occurring: loss of sea ice, accelerated sea level rise and longer, more intense heat waves. [2]

Climate change is fundamentally a social development issue. The impacts of a changing climate – including increases in extreme weather events and rising temperatures – are acute and multi-dimensional, already affecting vulnerabilities, resilience and social inequities globally, and placing lives and livelihoods at risk. There is a consensus in the literature that climate change will have far-reaching consequences for social development goals and economic development more broadly, including poverty reduction, food and nutrition security, economic growth, gender equality, social equity, and health. Moreover, causes and consequences of climate change are linked with global patterns of inequality and social justice. Evidence indicates that climate change impacts are not borne equally – demographic and socioeconomic factors such as gender, age, livelihood strategies and poverty shape levels of exposure to climate change effects, vulnerability and resilience (Ribot, 2010; Lambrou & Nelson, 2010; Skinner, 2011). [3]

The treacherous and complicated link of climate change with other primary risks is explained by the United Nations High Commissioner for Refugees (UNHCR) cautioning that climate change and natural disasters can exacerbate threats that force people to flee within their country or across international borders. The interplay between climate, conflict, hunger, poverty and persecution creates increasingly complex emergencies. For example, food insecurity may become a major driver of conflicts and displacement. An international alliance of the United Nations, governmental and non-governmental agencies working to address the root causes of extreme hunger reported that conflict, weather extremes and economic turbulence contributed to several disturbing trends. The group reported that at the end of 2019, 135 million people across 55 countries and territories experienced acute food insecurity. In addition, 75 million children had stunted growth and 17 million suffered from wasting. These findings represented the highest level of acute food insecurity and malnutrition documented since the group's first report in 2017. Eighty per cent of the world's displaced populations were residing in these 55 countries or territories. [4]

Human Development Report 2019 of the United Nations Development Programme (UNDP) warns that poorer countries and poorer people will be hit earlier and harder due to the effects of climate change. Some countries could quite literally disappear. Of all climate change's disruptive effects, perhaps none is greater than that on future generations, which will shoulder the burden of previous generations' fossil fuel-dependent development pathways. As the set of climate change damages intersects all other sets connected to human development, climate positive action is considered the most critical factor to achieve sustainable human development.

Poverty

According to Mahatma Gandhi poverty is the worst form of violence. The World Bank graphically portrays, "Poverty is lack of shelter. Poverty is being sick and not being able to see a doctor. Poverty is not having access to school and not knowing how to read. Poverty is not having a job, is fear for the future, living one day at a time. Poverty is losing a child to illness brought about by unclean water. Poverty is powerlessness, lack of representation and freedom." And more importantly, it is a vicious cycle from which no person or community can escape easily and it continues for generations.

Well into the 21ˢᵗ century hunger is still the world's biggest health problem. And it is about to get worse. Around 9 million people die every year of hunger and hunger-related diseases. This is more than from AIDS, malaria and tuberculosis combined. Poor nutrition and hunger are responsible for the death of 3.1 million children a year. That is nearly half of all deaths in children under the age of 5. The children die because their bodies lack basic nutrients. Globally, 822 million people suffer from undernourishment. The number of people affected by hunger has decreased by 189 million people since 1990. But in recent years the positive development has stopped. Since 2015, we have seen an increase in hungry people globally every year. The number of people affected by hunger is the highest in the African continent where 20% of the population don't get enough to eat. In parts of eastern and southern Africa, the number is over 30%. In Sub-Saharan Africa, 1 in 3 children experience stunted growth because they don't get enough food or vitamins. Besides a number of health issues, stunted growth also affects the children's cognitive abilities. Of the 822 million undernourished people in the world, 113 million face acute hunger meaning they are in urgent need of food and nutrients. 24% of the world population live in areas of food insecurity. 9% in areas of severe food insecurity. These numbers could very well go up as climate change increasingly affects the global food systems. Falling food production is a likely consequence of higher CO2 concentrations in the atmosphere, higher temperatures and increased water scarcity. In 2017, over 20 million people in the African countries of Ethiopia, Malawi, Zimbabwe, and Kenya experienced acute food insecurity as a consequence of climate change. While 822 million people suffer from undernourishment, about a third of all food for human consumption is lost or wasted. [5]

According to the latest World Bank report on poverty, the global extreme poverty rate fell to 9.2 percent in 2017, from 10.1 percent in 2015. That is equivalent to 689 million people living on less than $1.90 a day. At higher poverty lines, 24.1 percent of the world lived on less than $3.20 a day and 43.6 percent on less than $5.50 a day in 2017.

In 2018, four out of five people below the international poverty line lived in rural areas. Half of the poor are children. Women represent a majority of the poor in most regions and among same age groups. About 70 percent of the global poor aged 15 and over have no schooling or only some basic education. Almost half of poor people in Sub-Saharan Africa live in just five countries: Nigeria, the Democratic Republic of Congo, Tanzania, Ethiopia, and Madagascar. More than 40 percent of the global poor live in economies affected by fragility, conflict and violence, and that number is expected to rise to 67 percent in the next decade. Those economies have just 10 percent of the world's population. About 132 million of the global poor live in areas with high flood risk.

For the first time in a generation, the quest to end poverty has suffered its worst setback. Global extreme poverty is expected to rise in 2020 for the first time in over 20 years as the disruption of the COVID-19 pandemic compounds the forces of conflict and climate change, which were already slowing poverty reduction progress. Many people who had barely escaped extreme poverty could be forced back into it by the convergence of COVID-19, conflict, and climate change. A "nowcast" (preliminary estimate) for 2020, incorporating the effects of the COVID-19 pandemic, projects that an additional 88 million to 115 million people will be pushed into extreme poverty, bringing the total to between 703 and 729 million. Middle-income countries such as India and Nigeria will be significantly affected; middle-income countries may be home to 82% of the new poor. The newest and most immediate threat to poverty reduction, COVID-19, has unleashed a worldwide economic disaster whose shock waves continue to spread. Without an adequate global response, the cumulative effects of the pandemic and its economic fallout, armed conflict, and climate change will exact high human and economic costs well into the future. [6]

Poverty attacks physical and psychological status of a person very badly like nothing else. Risk factors of poverty are, emotional and social challenges, acute and chronic stressors, cognitive lags and health and safety issues. The aggregate of risk factors makes everyday living a struggle; they are multifaceted and interwoven, building on and playing off one another with a devastatingly synergistic effect. In other words, one problem created by poverty begets another, which in turn contributes to another, leading to a seemingly endless cascade of deleterious consequences. [7]

Without outside intervention, one cannot escape from the vicious cycle of poverty. Money alone cannot alleviate poverty. Providing access to basic education, sanitation and health facilities, safe drinking water, electricity, technology etc., to the poor only will enable them to break the cycle of poverty. The World Social Summit identified poverty eradication as an ethical, social, political and economic imperative of mankind and called on governments to address the root causes of poverty, provide for basic needs for all and ensure that the poor have access to productive resources, including credit, education and training. A social perspective on development requires addressing poverty in all its dimensions. It promotes people-centred approach to poverty eradication advocating the empowerment of people living in poverty through their full participation in all aspects of political, economic and social life, especially in the design and implementation of policies that affect the poorest and most vulnerable groups of society. An integrated strategy towards poverty eradication necessitates implementing policies geared to more equitable distribution of wealth and income and social protection coverage.

In one year period of current pandemic, about 2.6 million people have died of corona virus across the world. It is also a fact that on an average about 9 million poor die **every year** due to hunger and malnutrition. Ironically, COVID-19 threatened the entire world, from presidents to priests and halted all human as well as gods' activities for few months, causing an unprecedented global economic and spiritual crisis. The entire media focused its prime coverage on this pandemic and no person on earth is unaware of this health issue. On the contrary, hardly a few thousand people living in developing and developed nations may be aware of the fact of mass deaths by hunger every year which is about 3 times of the number of people died of coronavirus. Ever sensational media gives the least attention to issues relating to poverty and hunger deaths, as it involves poor who according to their assessment do not matter in the world. Life and death are same for every person. But its value is different for different classes of people! This reflects the present status of collective consciousness of humanity in the so-called highly civilized world!!

Inequality

Inequality refers to disparities and discrepancies in areas such as income, wealth, education, health, nutrition, space, politics, social identity etc. Inequality of opportunities refers to differences in people's background or circumstances that condition what they are able to achieve. Global inequality refers to difference in income between all individuals in the world rather than inequalities between countries. Among all inequalities, economic inequality impacts the human development seriously. Accomplishment of reasonable economic equality in a community would invalidate the effects of other forms of inequalities. Increasing gap in economic inequality which is an inevitable outcome of growth in economy means differential access to wealth and income among the population of a country and between countries. This inequality is gaining the major attention of the world economists and policy makers as the present market economy continues to facilitate the accumulation of wealth and income in fewer hands while keeping about 10% of the world population under extreme poverty conditions.

The world added 8 billionaires a week in 2020 – 421 in a year – taking their total number to a record 3,288, according to the 10th Edition of Hurun Global Rich List 2021 released in March 2021. Despite the COVID-19 pandemic, the total wealth of all billionaires across the globe surged 32 per cent during the period under review to $14.7 trillion. "Billionaires have added in the past year the equivalent of the gross domestic product (GDP) of Germany to take their wealth to the equivalent of China. They added $3.5 trillion to take their total wealth to $14.7 trillion, a huge concentration of economic power," the report said. India, which stands at 131st position among the 189 countries ranked in Human Development Index 2020, retained its third spot in the ranking of country of billionaires with a total of 177 billionaires living in the country. The above facts and figures provide a real picture of reckless concentration of wealth in the hands of few individuals and the fast and unprecedented widening gap in economic inequality within and between the states.

Poverty and prosperity are two ends of the elastic band of economic inequality. This band of inequality will remain elastic as long as it preserves social cohesions in the prevailing socioeconomic conditions of the society to enable to encourage professionalism and entrepreneurship, trigger competition, and sustain overall economic growth. If the ends of the band are stretched too far, the desired result of elasticity would be lost and the political, economic, and socio-cultural fabric of the society would get damaged and torn out. Such delicate political and socio-economic conditions only contribute to the outbursts of people in many parts of the world demanding jobs, price reduction, good governance etc. Economic liberalism and globalization trends of recent decades facilitated unprecedented and unrestricted accumulation of wealth and income in the hands of very few individuals. This fast and unimaginable change in the differential measure of inequality range indicates that we are at the critical threshold of crossing the limit of elasticity. Further, inequality among countries and societies impacts the opportunities of individuals in accessing good education, health and technology, which in turn leads to internal and international conflicts.

A World Bank report of 2018 found that global wealth grew an estimated 66 percent (from $690 trillion to $1,143 trillion in constant 2014 U.S. dollars at market prices). But inequality was substantial, as wealth per capita in high-income OECD countries was 52 times greater than in low-income countries. According to Credit Suisse Global Wealth Report-2019, bottom half of wealth holders collectively accounted for less than 1% of total global wealth in mid-2019, while the richest 10% own 82% of global wealth and the top 1% alone own 45%. Oxfam's 2020 report says that 2,153 billionaires owned as much wealth as the bottom 4.6 billion people in 2019. The gap of inequality keeps widening due to globalization, free market economy, recent advancements in technology, digitization, e-commerce etc. Economist Thomas Piketty asserts that widening economic disparity is an inevitable phenomenon of free market capitalism when the rate of return of capital (r) is greater than the rate of growth of the economy. [8] The GDP growth rate in developed countries hovered around 2% prior to coronavirus pandemic and now except China all other countries are recording negative GDP growth. But the rate of profit of the multinational business entities gained from recent global spurt in economy, located in these countries are many times higher than their national average GDP growth rate. Resultantly, there is faster accumulation of wealth in the hands of top business people of developed and developing nations.

Inequality is a fundamental issue for human development. Extreme inequalities in opportunity and life chance have a direct bearing on human capabilities. Deep human development disparities persist between rich people and poor people, men and women, rural and urban areas and different regions and groups. These inequalities create mutually reinforcing structures of disadvantage that follow people through life cycles and are transmitted across generations. This is wrong for both intrinsic and instrumental reasons. Inequality violates basic precepts of social justice, but it is also bad for growth, bad for democracy and bad for social cohesion. [9]

Going beyond the conventional factors of inequality, the HDR 2019 report articulates on the rise of a new generation of inequalities with reference to human development in the 21st century. This report gives the following key findings: -

1. Disparities in human development remain widespread, despite achievements in reducing extreme deprivations.

2. A new generation of inequalities is emerging, with divergence in enhanced capabilities, despite convergence in basic capabilities.

3. Inequalities accumulate through life, often reflecting deep power imbalances.

4. Assessing and responding to inequalities in human development demands a revolution in metrics.

5. We can redress inequalities if we act now, before imbalances in economic power are politically entrenched. [10]

Besides poverty, the reason why inequality is considered as a critical global risk is that poverty is mostly location based and static, whereas the accelerating and widening spectrum of inequality is dynamic and has global implications. Its immediate impact on the common people disturbs the social, economic and political order, which in turn disrupts human development process. Anticipating this kind of situation, Bill Gates urged upon the youngsters a decade ago, addressing them, "Humanity's greatest advances are not in its discoveries – but in how those discoveries are applied to reduce inequity. Whether through democracy, strong public education, quality health care, or broad economic opportunity – reducing inequity is the highest human achievement." [11]

Large Scale and Religious Armed Conflicts

Armed conflicts, particularly in fragile and less developed countries have remained a major hurdle in the human development of extremely poor people living in these countries. These conflicts do not spare civilians and the violence they face due to the conflicts make their poverty conditions further worse. Globally, the absolute number of war deaths has been declining since 1946. And yet, internal conflict and violence are currently on the rise, with many conflicts today waged on sectarian and religious grounds mostly by non-state actors such as political militias, criminals, and international terrorist groups. Unresolved regional and religious tensions, breakdown in the rule of law, absent or co-opted state institutions, illicit economic gain, and the scarcity of resources exacerbated by climate change, have become dominant drivers of conflict. [12]

Conflicts in developing and under-developed countries are on the raise since 1950. Wars in these countries often have cultural dimensions related to ethnicity or religion, but there are invariably underlying economic causes too. Major root causes include political, economic, and social inequalities; extreme poverty; economic stagnation; poor government services; high unemployment; environmental degradation; and individual (economic) incentives to fight. Wars are a major cause of poverty, underdevelopment, and ill health in poor countries. To reduce the likelihood of wars it is essential to promote inclusive development; reduce inequalities between groups; tackle unemployment; and, via national and international control over illicit trade, reduce private incentives to fight. [13]

The most alarming human crisis in the past decades remains forced migration of people including children, women and aged, due to armed ethnic and religious conflicts. Recently, the world's focus has been on the Rohingya crisis in Myanmar, with nearly 75% of the country's Muslim population fleeing to neighbouring Bangladesh in the wake of violence and ethnic cleansing. In 2017, amid the escalation of ongoing tension and violence, the United Nations deemed the plight of the Rohingya the "fastest-growing refugee emergency" in the world. Forced migration has been a norm in the Middle East for most of the 21st Century, according to Oxford University's Refugee Studies Centre. Syria's deadly civil war has caused over 11 million instances of forced migration. To-date nearly 6.2 million Syrians are internally displaced, and over 5.6 million Syrians are counted as refugees. The Democratic Republic of Congo has the highest number of displaced people on the continent of Africa, with nearly 6 million people forced from their homes by various conflicts. South Sudan has been continuously plagued by war-induced migration during its short existence. [14] A surge in violent conflict since 2010 has led to historically high levels of forced displacement. Globally, there are about 79.5 million forcibly displaced people who have fled their homes to escape violence, conflict and persecution. [15]

The hardships endured through the displacement have made the poor more vulnerable. They are forced to lose their assets and livelihoods, and hence unable to plan their future. Many suffer from trauma, and women and girls are at high risk of gender-based violence. They need help to regain their status and begin rebuilding their lives. Host communities need support, too. The forcibly displaced often live in poor areas in developing countries that are struggling to meet their own development goals. Accommodating the sudden arrival of masses of newcomers presents a challenge for host governments, putting further pressure on their ability to deliver basic services and infrastructure. This is why forced displacement is not only a humanitarian crisis, it is a development challenge as well. The large-scale and religious conflicts in fragile nations literally choke the human development activities in these countries and have spill-over effect on other nations too. Perpetration of violence on already poverty-stricken poor civilians and their large-scale displacement make the violent conflicts the world's worst cause responsible for the worst form of human sufferings.

UN'S HUMAN DEVELOPMENT TRACK

One of the Uniter Nation's (UN) central mandates is the promotion of higher standards of living, full employment, and conditions of economic and social progress and development. As much as 70 per cent of the work of the UN system is devoted to accomplishing this mandate with the hope that eradicating poverty and improving the well-being of people everywhere are necessary steps in creating conditions for lasting world peace. The UN has played a crucial role in building international consensus on action for development. Beginning in 1960, the General Assembly has helped set priorities and goals through a series of 10-year International Development Strategies. While focusing on issues of particular concern, the Decades have consistently stressed the need for progress on all aspects of social and economic development. The UN continues formulating new development objectives in such key areas as sustainable development, the advancement of women, human rights, environmental protection and good governance – along with programmes to make them a reality.

At the Millennium Summit in September 2000, world leaders adopted a set of Millennium Development Goals (MDGs) aimed at eradicating extreme poverty and hunger; achieving universal primary education; promoting gender equality and empowering women; reducing child mortality; improving maternal health; combating HIV/AIDS, malaria and other diseases; and ensuring environmental sustainability — through a set of measurable targets to be achieved by the year 2015. Among these are: cutting in half the proportion of those who earn less than a dollar a day; achieving universal primary education; eliminating gender disparity at all levels of education; and dramatically reducing child mortality while increasing maternal health.

In continuation of the efforts in achieving inclusive human development, 195 member nations of the United Nation resolved in 2015 to change the world for the better by targeting Seventeen Sustainable Development Goals (SDGs), which would be accomplished by bringing together their respective governments, businesses, media, institutions of higher education, and local NGOs, by the year 2030. The preamble of the agenda of the SDGs states, "This Agenda is a plan of action for people, planet and prosperity. It also seeks to strengthen universal peace in larger freedom. We recognise that eradicating poverty in all its forms and dimensions, including extreme poverty, is the greatest global challenge and an indispensable requirement for sustainable development. All countries and all stakeholders, acting in collaborative partnership, will implement this plan. We are resolved to free the human race from the tyranny of poverty and want and to heal and secure our planet. We are determined to take the bold and transformative steps which are urgently needed to shift the world onto a sustainable and resilient path. As we embark on this collective journey, we pledge that no one will be left behind. The 17 Sustainable Development Goals and 169 targets which we are announcing today demonstrate the scale and ambition of this new universal Agenda.

They seek to build on the Millennium Development Goals and complete what these did not achieve. They seek to realize the human rights of all and to achieve gender equality and the empowerment of all women and girls. They are integrated and indivisible and balance the three dimensions of sustainable development: the economic, social and environmental. The Goals and targets will stimulate action over the next fifteen years in areas of critical importance for humanity and the planet." [16] Many agencies of the UN are vigorously pursuing the SDGs.

A study made in 2018 to assess the achievement of the MDGs revealed that most of the UN's development goals were missed. However, the world achieved three and a half targets: MDG Target 1.A – halving the share of the world population living in extreme poverty – is a particularly important one and while most people are not aware of it, the world has actually achieved this goal. The achievement of MDG 3 meant that the gender disparity in education was closed at the global level. And MDG Target 6.C on malaria and tuberculosis was achieved as the world was able to reduce the global rate of new infections. For MDG 7 the world achieved half of this goal – while the goal for sanitation was missed, the world did reach the goal on providing access to safe drinking water. [17]

Executive Summary of Sustainable Development Report 2019 which reviewed the performance of 193 countries in reaching the 17 Sustainable Development Goals (SDGs) reports that no country is on track for achieving all the 17 goals with major performance gaps even in the top countries on SDG 12 (Responsible Consumption and Production), SDG 13 (Climate Action), SDG 14 (Life Below Water) and SDG 15 (Life on Land). Income and wealth inequalities, as well as gaps in health and education outcomes by population groups also remain important policy challenges in developing and developed countries alike. High-level political commitment to the SDGs is falling short of historic promises. Out of 43 countries surveyed on SDG implementation efforts, including all G20 countries and countries with a population greater than 100 million, 33 countries have endorsed the SDGs in official statements since January 1st, 2018. Yet in only 18 of them, central budget documents mention the SDGs. Trends on climate (SDG 13) and biodiversity (SDG 14 and SDG 15) are alarming. On average, countries obtain their worst scores on SDG 13 (Climate Action), SDG 14 (Life Below Water) and SDG 15 (Life on Land). No country obtains a "green rating" (synonym of SDG achieved) on SDG 14 (Life Below Water). Trends on greenhouse gas emissions and, even more so, on threatened species are moving in the wrong direction. These findings are in line with the recent reports from the Intergovernmental Panel on Climate Change (IPCC) and the Intergovernmental Science-Policy Platform on Biodiversity and Ecosystem Services (IPBES) on climate change mitigation and biodiversity protection, respectively. High-income countries generate high environmental and socio-economic spill-over effects. Domestic implementation of the SDGs should not undermine other countries' ability to achieve the goals. Eradicating poverty and strengthening equity remain important policy priorities. Eradicating extreme poverty remains a global challenge with half of the world's nations not on track for achieving the SDG 1 (No Poverty). [18]

The above facts indicate that many countries have not taken the threats of global risks, including the climate change seriously and do not bother much about the sustainable and inclusive human development of the world community. While some states are hesitant to take actions as planned to reach SDGs in their respective countries, a few nations disrupt the efforts of other countries in reaching their targets. If the states which are supposed to protect and promote the collective interests of their citizens and the global community as well are unable to or disinclined to perform their internationally agreed basic obligations to ensure a peacefully sustainable world, then there should be something fundamentally wrong with their constitution and behaviour.

WHERE DO WE GO WRONG?

Thanks to the long strides of progress made in science and technology in recent decades, now we understand from sub-atomic particles to the formation of universe. We have progressed from DNA decoding to cloning to bioprinting organs. Today, we are in digital age, aided by automation, artificial intelligence, satellite aided communication, quantum computers etc. Machines can talk to each other and human voice and brain can communicate with machines now. Most of the public and private services have become digital enabling faster and easier delivery of services and goods to public. Information and communication technology and faster transport facilities have shrunk the world into a global village. The recently evolved concept of work from home due to coronavirus pandemic has further changed the dimensions of space and time. These innovative and fast changing technological advancements in the past three decades have suddenly increased the production of goods in quantum levels and the digital technology has enabled global markets for such mass-produced goods and integrated services by e-commerce. These developments coupled with globalization have contributed to the fastest ever growth of the global wealth in the history and more particularly, income and wealth of industrialized nations have increased exponentially in the recent past. At the same time, such incredible advancements made in science and technology and unprecedented growth in global wealth have not helped to eliminate the extreme poverty conditions of millions of people completely and permanently. From this, it is evident that the epoch-making evolution made in the fields of science, technology, medicine, agriculture etc., are not utilized optimally to support the efforts of human development. Else, one in every ten people of the world would not suffer extreme poverty, 76 million people would not languish in 37 Fragile and Conflict Affected Countries (FAC), 9 million people would not die of hunger every year and two-thirds of the global population (4 billion people) live under conditions of severe water scarcity at least 1 month of the year.

Now the COVID-19 pandemic out-break has questioned the efficacy of global governance, exposed the limitation of international institutions and the inability of many governments to handle the crisis. This panicky situation has created mistrust and tension among nations and thereby accelerated the momentum in the already commenced de-globalization trend supported by rising populistic ideologies. Consequently, the new political and economic world order that may emerge after the pandemic is likely to be characterized by intense nationalism and protectionism, giving scant attention to global common good, like climate justice and sustainable human development. The attempt to address the global risks and make the world a safer place has now become more difficult than ever before.

As discussed above, the United Nations and its various organizations have prioritized and formulated well-structured human development goals as MDGs and SDGs with pragmatic targets to achieve a better and more sustainable world for all. Even with the background and the experience of running welfare programs, many governments are either not able or reluctant to achieve the targets of the current SD Goals. Ironically, majority of the developed and developing nations including rich people living there are eager to eliminate poverty everywhere, take faster climate positive action and live in a peaceful environment. There is no dearth of materials, human resources, technology and ideas to execute the action plan towards achieving these goals. To some extent, there is political will also in many countries to achieve the SDGs. Then what could be the barriers that hold back governments, international institutions, voluntary organizations and activists from achieving such well formulated and astutely targeted goals to build a safe, peaceful, reasonably equitable and sustainable world for now and the future? This book attempts to find answers to this question with a new political perspective, besides discussing some pragmatic and logical solutions to fix the problems.

CONGENITAL AND BEHAVIOURAL DISORDERS OF STATE

State is the key political instrument responsible for addressing the global risks and human development problems of its citizens. Of the 193 member nations of the UN, about 45 - 55 are currently considered as fragile and conflict affected states, where the majority of the population live in impoverished conditions. Since the administrative machinery of the government is weak in these countries, it is not easy to implement the human development programmes either by the state or external agencies. Therefore, extreme poverty continues to persist in these countries for long, entrapped in a vicious cycle. On the other side, developed states are not willing to achieve the SDGs related to climate positive action and in the process of achieving the remaining goals, they disrupt other countries in achieving their SDGs. Former US President Donald Trump decided to leave the Paris Climate Agreement relating to climate action and also announced to quit the World Health Organization (WHO). It is apparent that though agreed universally, there is no positive intention among many signatory states of the UN resolution to achieve the SDGs by 2030 and some states are incapable of achieving the goals. Further, there is lack of continuity and uniformity among many nations in taking action as scheduled by the UNDP to achieve the SD Goals. Studies made on the progress of MDGs and SDGs analyse the structural, functional and policy deficiencies of the states in reaching the targets. These are symptomatic shortcomings of states which keep changing, as the governments change as in the case of the US recently and as their geopolitical strategy and socioeconomic conditions change. But no study has so far been done to go into the root of the problems of such deficient and delinquent behaviour of states that do not bother about the welfare of their own as well as global community. However, such a study is not possible in absence of a universal voluntary or regulatory framework for all states (except the weak UN and its agencies) committed or mandated to a minimum standard of human development or the essential common good of the global community. Hence, the states can defy the consensus or deviate from the agreed plan of action towards reaching the sustainable development goals or any other international agreement made in the interest of common good of the international community with impunity. This kind of irresponsible and deranged behaviour reflecting the constitutional and functional weakness of state are the root cause of all the hurdles in addressing the global risks and achieving the SDGs. This problem actually originated from the birth of the political concept of sovereign state in Europe about four centuries ago with '**congenital disorder**' and later it got complicated by '**behavioural disorder**' acquired during its transition period from sovereign state to nation state, a century later.

Congenital Disorder of State

To bring an end to the Thirty Years War (1618–1648) fought in Europe on religious and other issues, two treaties, collectively called The Peace of Westphalia were signed in Germany in 1648. It introduced the abstract concept of absolute and independent sovereignty (supreme authority within a territory recognized by other states) for the first time to state political system, and by defining balance of power in Europe, laid down the foundation for international world order. Urgency and circumstances prevailed at the time of finalising the treaty led to a serious and permanent omission. When the interest of the Holy Roman Empire and other monarch rulers of Europe who were parties to the treaty were secured sufficiently with their power of independent sovereignty over demarcated territory, the citizens were deprived of their right to approve the validity of that authority. When the citizens living in a state territory were made to obey the rulers and the laws made by them compulsorily, there were no provisions made for them to approve or disapprove of the authority of such rulers. Consent of public for governance by any ruler is called political or state legitimacy of the government. There was no democratic political system like election in practice at the time of signing the treaty, which could have ensured the public approval of the authority to govern them. However, some other methodology, like prescription of certain process for the rulers to generate state legitimacy in an explicit manner could have been thought of and prescribed. Whatever be the circumstances, the treaty was one-sided and an important and lasting political contract was made between the rulers and the citizens without the consent of one party, i.e., the citizens. In result, the legally invalid and naturally flawed Westphalian state system that was conceptualised and introduced in Europe without integrating the essential element of political legitimacy in 17th century was accepted and adopted internationally and unfortunately, it continues to be followed till today without any change. This crucial omission and deficiency occurred at the time of conceiving the Westphalian state system is termed as **"congenital disorder of state"** and the symptoms of this disorder continue to manifest from its birth to till date. Presently, the political legitimacy of about 45–55 governments of fragile and conflict affected countries and few authoritarian states of the world, which are run by weak, ineffective, despotic and opaque governments is very much doubtful and the state legitimacy of quite a number of dubious democratic countries is also questionable.

Behavioural Disorder of State

Well after a century of the birth of Westphalian state system in Europe, in the pretext of promoting the motto of the French Revolution (1789), Napoleon consolidated the people of France introducing the idea of 'nationalism' unintentionally and tried to expand the rule of France in Europe, which resulted in the formation of 'nation state' in France. Later, the concept of nationalism spread in Europe and new nation states were formed based on national group identities like commonly shared ethnicity, history, religion, language, culture etc., for claiming the legitimacy to rule the nation state of that group by elites of the society replacing monarchs. Armed with such nationalistic principles, the nation states crossed their borders either to expand their territory to consolidate the people of their identity or to protect the people of their national identity living in other countries, deviating from the principle (sovereignty) of non-interference in the domestic and international matters of other states, laid down in the Westphalian state system. The idea of nationalism was so attractive and convincing to the citizens of the nation states, that they also acquired the identity and character of their respective nations and passionately involved themselves in the consolidation or expansionist activities of their country, reflecting their irrational behaviour. In fact, no such complete and voluntary cohesion and homogeneity of an identified group existed among all citizens of a nation state at any point of time from the birth of nation state in late 18ᵗʰ century to till date. Under the pride of nationalism, people started loving and caring for their identified group of fellow citizens. On contentious issues, they opposed fellow citizens who belong to other groups and hate citizens of other nations. This new trend of differentiating 'we' from 'others' introduced by the new concept of nationalism at the end of 18ᵗʰ century in Europe has been kept alive through the ages by the rulers in many counties of the world to gain political power and legitimacy, notwithstanding the tension and conflicts such divisions created, locally and internationally. This imaginary, mythical and emotional concept of nationalism and its manifestation of abnormal behaviour in the form of extreme patriotism, xenophobia, expansionism, racism etc., that had affected the psyche of nation state and its citizens is diagnosed as the **"behavioural disorder of state"**. This behavioural disorder led to two World Wars, a few violent totalitarian and racist regimes and many ethnic and religious wars of the past and that are still going on. This disorder is now associated with national populism identified with different set of characters and symptoms.

Need to Treat the Disorders

With a closer observation of the present world affairs, one can notice that citizens of many countries are living in a politically unhealthy conditions disabled by the above described congenital and behavioural disorders of state. Governing persons/body of many states are neither committed and accountable to their own citizens nor commonly agreed international framework and programmes for the common good of global community. There are states with fraudulent elections and pseudo democracy. Some states are run by theocratic, authoritarian and opaque governments. Violent conflicts and civil wars are going on in many countries due to nationalistic elements of ethnic, religious and sectarian divisions and rivalries. All failed, weak, fragile and conflict afflicted states are governed by the rulers with partial or no political legitimacy. Here people suffer from extreme poverty to forced migration. There are few countries run with neo-nationalistic ideologies that are against international liberalism, pluralism, multiculturalism, globalization, immigration, environmentalism and many other progressive ideas and harmless minority groups. These debilitating political conditions created by lack of state legitimacy, nationalistic rivalries and populist policies obstruct the flow of the benefits of scientific and technological advancements accomplished by the mankind so far and consequent growth in global economic opportunities to reach the poor living in underprivileged communities. Many political scientists and development economists who study weak, failed and fragile and conflict afflicted states have concurred on the fact that human development activities are not possible in the prevailing chaotic conditions of such states. With little scrutiny, it can be noticed that the root cause of such messy political and economic conditions that hamper the progress of human civilization are the congenital and behavioural disorders of state. With many states suffering from these disorders, it is very difficult to address the global risks and achieve sustainable human development goals, despite the advancements we have made in all fields of human endeavour, from agriculture to astronomy.

However, majority of the states have ingrained their presence strongly in the world political order and quite a few of them have recovered from these problems and show no sign of any symptoms of disorders. For centuries, the Westphalian state system has been taken for granted, and no other alternate model to state system has been proposed or experimented. State has become an inevitable political organ in the world political order and therefore, stateless society is not conceivable at this stage, as envisaged by Marxists and Anarchists. Alternatively, it may be possible to remove the systemic discrepancies of state by introducing historically missing and positively self-regulating elements in the psychic and the organic functions of the state and thereby making it responsible and accountable for the common good of local as well as global community.

2

CONGENITAL AND BEHAVIOURAL DISORDERS OF MODERN STATES

EVOLUTION OF WESTPHALIAN STATE SYSTEM

States and Maps

School kids memorizing names of countries and their capitals from world political map generally assume that these nations are in existence since time immemorial. When Kim Jong-un, Supreme Leader of North Korea and Donald Trump, ex-President of the USA argued on Twitter at the beginning of 2018 as to whose nuclear button is bigger, easily accessible and working, it appeared that they have not grown from this kiddish outlook. While bragging about the tools to destroy this planet which is 4.5 billion years old, they might not be conscious of the fact that the seed for the growth of present political system of "modern nation state" which they zealously represent was sown on earth just 370 years back only.

When foraging humans started to settle at a fixed place after their venture into agriculture and rearing domestic animals mostly on the banks of rivers, their cognizant ability matured, and invented script and money and introduced the ideas of polytheistic religion and political authority about 5000 years ago. Initially, a ruler had authority over the tribe which he belongs to, living in a small territory mainly to protect the lives and property of members of the tribe. Later the political concept of state was evolved slowly in tandem with the growth in human civilization, economy, culture, religions, civics etc.

It may seem very natural now to view the entire world as neatly divided into number of states as they appear on political maps of the world. But the division of the world into a collection of such states is less than 400 years old. Prior to the 1800's, the Earth's surface was organized in other ways, such as tribes, city-states, empires, and kingdoms. In addition, much of the earth's territory until very recently consisted of frontier regions that were not politically organized at all.

City-States

State is generally defined as a politically organized territory with a permanent population, a defined territory, sovereignty (the right to control its territory), and recognition by other states. The development of states can be traced to the ancient Middle East, in an area known as the Fertile Crescent. The eastern end of the Fertile Crescent was located in the valley between the Tigris and Euphrates rivers, in present day Iraq. The first states to evolve were the city-states in Mesopotamia and Greece. A city state is a sovereign state that comprises a town and the surrounding countryside. Walls clearly delineated the boundaries of the city, and outside the walls the city controlled agricultural land which supported the urban residents and provided the city-state with an outer line of defence against attack by other city-states. Vast undefined frontier regions separated these ancient city-states from one another.

Empires

Periodically one city-state would gain military dominance over the others and form an empire. An empire is a territory in which a central power extends its control over "weaker" areas and rules them as colonies. In the ancient Middle East, the dominant central power exerting its influence over a broad area was typically the dominant city-state. The boundaries of these empires, sometimes marked by walls, were imposed on distant frontier regions, often ignoring local conditions in those areas. But vast frontier regions still existed both within and between these empires. In the flux of time, the ancient Middle East came to be organized into a succession of such empires by the Sumerians, Assyrians, Babylonians, Persians, Egyptians, Greeks, and finally the Romans, under whom the political unity of ancient world reached its peak at the beginning of the common era (AD).

Kingdoms

When the Roman Empire collapsed in the fifth century, its European territories fragmented into a complicated patchwork of estates, many with poorly defined borders, ruled by competing kings, dukes, barons, and other nobles. Beginning around the year 1100, a handful of powerful kings gained control over many of these previously fragmented estates unifying them into kingdoms. A kingdom is a territory defined by the people's allegiance to a king. Though not yet legally or universally recognized, vague boundaries began to emerge between these European kingdoms thus reducing the size and number of undefined frontier areas. This consolidation of neighbouring estates under the control of kings formed the basis of the development of such modern states as England, France, and Spain. But even in the case of the early medieval kingdoms of England, France, and Spain, there was not yet a collective agreement among these rulers as to how these territories would be organized (territoriality) and what they could or could not do within their respective domains (sovereignty). Moreover, much of Central Europe--notably present-day Germany and Italy remained fragmented into large number estates that were not consolidated into states till the nineteenth century.

The Peace of Westphalia

The event in European history that marks the beginning of the state system is the Peace of Westphalia. The notorious Thirty Years War (1618 – 1648) or series of connected wars began in 1618 in Europe, when the Austrian

Habsburgs tried to impose Roman Catholicism on their Protestant subjects in Bohemia. This pitted the Protestants against the Catholics, the Holy Roman Empire against France, the German princes and princelings against the emperor and each other, and France against the Habsburgs of Spain. The Swedes, the Danes, the Poles, the Russians, the Dutch and the Swiss were all dragged in or dived in. Commercial interests and rivalries played a part, as did religion and power politics. About eight million people (a quarter of the population) died in this bloody war. After prolonged negotiations of peace among various parties of the disputes, treaties were signed in 1648 in the Westphalian towns of Germany (Münster and Osnabrück), which are collectively called The Peace of Westphalia to bring an end to the already ongoing Eighty Years' War between Spain and the Dutch and the German phase of the Thirty Years' War.

Westphalian State System

The rise of the Westphalian state system marked a fundamental change in the relationship between people and territory. Before Westphalia, one's loyalty was to a king or religious head or other local ruler and that ruler's territory comprised of any area inhabited by his loyal subjects. Boundaries were poorly defined because loyalties could change frequently from one ruler to another. To the extent that people had mixed loyalties, the territory ruled by different kings could overlap. In a sense, before Westphalia, loyalty defined territory. After the Peace of Westphalia, however, territory defined the loyalty. Now the population living in a territory have to obey the ruler having sovereignty over that territory. In theory, after Westphalia there were no longer overlapping areas of power or loyalty.

The Peace of Westphalia firmed up the political structure of state by introducing hitherto unknown political concepts of state sovereignty and balance of power in Europe. The peace of Westphalia became a turning point in the history of nations because the elements it set in place were as uncomplicated as they were sweeping. The state, not the empire, dynasty, or religious confession, was affirmed as the building block of European order. The concept of state sovereignty was established. The right of each signatory to choose its own domestic structure and religious orientation free from intervention was affirmed, while novel clauses ensured that minority sects could practice their faith in peace and be free from the prospect of forced conversion. [1]

CONGENITAL DISORDER OF STATE

The Peace of Westphalia empowered the rulers affirming fixed territory, presumed political legitimacy, universally recognized sovereignty and authority to rule the population living in that territory. It was negotiated in the context of the then prevailing political conditions of Europe without the idea and intention of creating a universally applicable political system for the future and hence the rulers in the rest of the world were not involved in the negotiations. Fixed territory in place of loyalty of the citizens to define the jurisdiction of the power of a ruler and the new political concept of state sovereignty brought in new European political order and consolidated the power of rulers delinking the state from the control of the Pope. This inspired the rulers of other parts of the world also to adopt the principles of Westphalian state system in their respective regions/states willingly.

In political science, legitimacy is the right and acceptance of an authority, usually a governing law or a regime. Whereas authority denotes a specific position in an established government, the term legitimacy denotes a system of government—wherein government denotes "sphere of influence". An authority viewed as legitimate often has the right and justification to exercise power. Political legitimacy is considered a basic condition for governing, without which a government will suffer legislative deadlock(s) and collapse. [2]

State legitimacy is an age-old political principle first enunciated by Aristotle arguing that the legitimacy of the government relies upon constitutionalism and consent and he posits that political stability relies upon the legitimacy of rewards. Historically, very important political philosophies emerged in the Age of Enlightenment (17th &18th centuries), many of which emphasised the importance of participation of citizens in the state's formation and functioning. The Enlightenment-era British social philosopher John Locke (1632–1704) holds that political legitimacy derives from popular explicit and implicit consent of the governed. The English philosopher Thomas Hobbes ushered in this new debate with his work Leviathan in 1651. Hobbes also developed some of the fundamentals of European liberal thought: the right of the individual; the natural equality of all men; the artificial character of the political order (which led to the later distinction between civil society and the state); the view that all legitimate political power must be «representative» and based on the consent of the people. [3]

The Peace of Westphalia was signed in the middle of the 17th century, when the Age of Enlightenment began to blossom in Europe with political theories that focussed on citizens' political role and their rights in the functions of government and affairs of the state. Despite the importance given to state legitimacy in the past and the then emerging western political philosophies, the crucial element of political legitimacy was ignored to be considered while framing the Westphalian state system in 1648. This led the monarchs and kings to claim their power and authority to rule their citizens with inherent legitimacy claimed to be derived from the 'Divine right' that was supported by religious establishments.

The Westphalian state system had not prescribed the modalities of creating a legal bond between the rulers and their citizens (who so far enjoyed the freedom of choosing their ruler with their choice of loyalty); however, the citizens were made to obey the law of the state. It failed to enumerate the essential duties of the rulers and their responsibility and accountability towards citizens. Citizens' natural and legal rights were not safeguarded. Besides the concept of mutual recognition of state's sovereignty, the treaties did not lay down any obligations like ensuring the common good of the people of the state or the whole of Europe. There was no methodology prescribed for the rulers to generate and demonstrate their political legitimacy in any manner. Similarly, the citizens also had no way to express their approval or disapproval of the authority of the rulers to govern them. It was like a contract without mutual consent and agreement. But this contract empowered the rulers enormously, whereas it deprived the citizens of their basic political rights. From the conception of the idea of Westphalian state, these uneven features in favour of the rulers, embedded by the Peace of Westphalia have continued to prevail till now. The UN Charter does not prescribe a minimum degree of political legitimacy of a state to enrol as its member. Governments of many states take advantage of this weakness in the concept of Westphalian state system and rule the countries with no or insufficient or false legitimacy, slowly making the states dysfunctional and pushing the millions of their citizens to the brink of inhuman conditions (e.g.-Sub-Saharan states). In some states, this unbridled power makes the rulers tyrannical and they go to the extent of treating their own citizens with cruelty (e.g.- Hitler's Germany and the present North Korea and Syria). Even after the introduction of democracy, a political system in which a government can legally generate its political legitimacy by way of conducting elections, many states are reluctant to follow this system, as the Westphalian state system does not mandate political legitimacy (e.g.- China & Middle Eastern states). A recent study revealed that full democracy thrives in about 23 countries of the world only. The present state of affairs shows that even after 370 years of the birth of Westphalian state system and the introduction of democracy and election, the rulers of huge majority of states are disinclined to prove their citizens and the world explicitly that they have the political legitimacy to rule the state. This critical omission to integrate the political legitimacy in the state system is playing havoc in the lives of billions of people of the world since the time of conception and birth of the Westphalian state system and this conceptual error committed at the time of the birth of sovereign state system is identified as '**Congenital Disorder**' of state.

Henry Kissinger addresses this congenital disorder stating that the Westphalian peace reflected a practical accommodation to reality, not a unique moral insight. It relied on a system of independent states refraining from interference in each other's domestic affairs and checking each other's ambitions through a general equilibrium of power. No single claim to truth or universal rule had prevailed in Europe's contests. Instead, each state was assigned the attribute of sovereign power over its territory. Each would acknowledge the domestic structures and religious vocations of its fellow states and refrain from challenging their existence. [4]

He goes on to say that the universal relevance of the Westphalian system derived from its procedural – that is, value—neutral – nature. Its rules are accessible to any country: non-interference in domestic affairs of other states; inviolability of borders; sovereignty of states; encouragements of international law. The weakness of the Westphalian system has been the reverse side its strength. Designed as it was by states exhausted from their bloodletting, it did not supply a sense of direction. It dealt with methods of allocating and preserving power; it gave no answer to the problem of how generate legitimacy. [5]

The major shortcoming of Westphalian state system is that it conferred unrestricted power and intrinsic legitimacy to the rulers without any kind of regulations or restrictions. It makes other states to recognize the sovereignty of a state irrespective of the fact whether such state is governed with sufficient political legitimacy or not. Therefore, there is no internal or external controls or restrictions for the authority of state. Historically and traditionally all games are played with rules. Any game played without rules is not a game. Even in the games involving fight between two persons, there are strict rules to be followed. For citizens of every state, there is no other entity more powerful and important to their life than their state. Such a powerful state which plays the most crucial role in the life of its every citizen is allowed to exercise its authority without any rules, limitations, framework and internal or external control or supervision. This dreadful omission committed while conceiving the static but still surviving Westphalian state system continues to haunt the world political order.

This primary weakness of the Westphalian state system discounts all other progress made by the mankind in science, technology and economy and block the benefits of such progress to reach a section of population living in fragile countries, particularly in some Sub-Saharan, South Asian and Latin American regions. Consequently, abject poverty remains and the gap in inequalities keeps widening and spreading across different states and communities under the nose of the much accomplished and filthy rich world.

EVOLUTION OF NATION STATE

Well after The Peace of Westphalia, absolutist rulers controlled these newly defined European states. During the latter part of the seventeenth and the eighteenth centuries, however, the development of an increasingly wealthy middle class proved to be the undoing of absolutism in parts of Western Europe. City-based merchants gained money, influence, and prestige. The traditional measure of affluence—land—became less important and the power of the nobility declined. These merchants and businesspeople demanded political recognition. In 1789, a democratic revolution in France, conducted in the name of the French people, ushered in an era in which the one's ultimate loyalty within a territory was seen as not to a hereditary monarch but rather to an imagined nation, a group of people who think of themselves as one based on a shared history and culture. Exactly how a nation is defined depends on how people see themselves as part of a nation. Nations may variously see themselves as sharing a religion, a language, an ethnicity, a religion, or, in the case of the United States, even a set of civic principles that tie them together.

With the French Revolution, the idea of the nation-state, a politically organized area in which a nation and state occupy the same space, became the aspiration of political elites around the world. The idea that the map of states should look like a map of nations was consciously promoted by European philosophers and elites as a way of controlling the sovereignty and territorial integrity of states after the fall of the monarchies in Europe.

The problem for these elites was that nation-states--well-defined, stable nations living within discrete territories--were an ideal that, then as now, did not actually exist.

In reality, all nations are ultimately mixtures of different peoples. The French are often considered to be the classic example of a nation, but France as a nation is very much an invention of the 18th and 19th century European elites. Only about 20% of the people living in France spoke French at the time of the French Revolution. Even the most French feeling person today is the product of a melding together of a wide variety of culture groups over time, including Celts, Ancient Romans, Franks, Goths, and many others. Nations are created, not naturally born of some distinct, mythical, primordial ancestral group, as claimed by the present neo-nationalists.

Since nation-states did not really exist, they had to be created to maintain territorial integrity. In some cases, this meant privileging one ethnic group at the expense of others. In other cases, it meant absorbing smaller entities into their borders. It often meant redrawing national borders to fit "nations", most often determined by language. But mostly the creation of nation-states took the form of an explicit attempt by elites to create a single national identity out of the diverse peoples within their borders. They did this by promoting a sense of shared history and culture (whether based on fact or not) through public education, and through the promotion of national languages and dictionaries, symbols, holidays, cemeteries, songs, and dress (the Scottish kilt was an invention of the 19th century Scottish nationalism).

Thus, cultivated by European elites in a century or so after the French Revolution, nationalism reached its peak in the nineteenth century. In some cases, the pursuit of nationalist ambitions produced greater cohesion in long-established states, such as in France and Spain. In other cases, nationalism became the rallying cry for bringing together people with some shared historical or cultural elements into a single state, as in the cases of Germany and Italy, both of which became states only at the end of the nineteenth century. Similarly, people who saw themselves as separate nations within other states launched successful separatist movements, as in Ireland, Poland, and Norway.

BEHAVIOURAL DISORDER OF STATE

The French Revolution was launched with the ideals of liberty, equality and fraternity which ultimately overthrew the monarchy and established a republic in France. Later it catalysed violent periods of political turmoil and finally culminated in a dictatorship under Napoleon. In the guise of spreading the ideals of revolution, he justified French expansionism and military campaigns, throwing the Westphalian principles of mutual recognition of sovereignty and non-interference in the domestic matters of other states to the wind. After Napoleon's defeat and downfall, French nationalism took on an assertive and extreme patriotism that supported military force to achieve its political goals. These violent and expansionist exploits of French nationalists in the name of the ideals of French Revolution exhibited the irrational behaviour of nation state at the nascent stage of its growth itself. After the fall and failure of over ambitious expansionists, Charles de Gaulle re-established democracy in France. He aptly said, "Patriotism is when love of your own people comes first; Nationalism, when hate for people other than your own comes first." [6]

Nationalism is inherently divisive because it highlights the perceived differences between people, emphasizing an individual's identification with their own nation. The idea is also potentially oppressive as it submerges individual identity within a national whole and gives elites or political leaders potential opportunities to manipulate or control the masses. According to Dr. Phil Kronk, a neuropsychologist, nationalism is a way of looking at yourself that comes from the identity only provided to you by your country. Your political, cultural and moral identities come from the nation to which you belong. A research paper on "National Identity and Mental Illness: The Double Helix of Modern Politics" presents the argument that certain forms of mental illness -- those today diagnosed as schizophrenia, manic depression, and major unipolar depression -- are products of the specific forms of identity and consciousness, associated with nationalism, and reflect the secular and egalitarian nature of national identity and national consciousness, which inevitably contribute to the creation of a relatively open, mobile society. The central values of nationalism (equality and popular sovereignty) encourage the individual to define oneself and thereby make such self-definition one's own responsibility. Personal identity-formation becomes problematic as a result, in a significant percentage of cases leading to a disordered sense of self -- the core symptom of these mental illnesses. [7]

Nationalism leads to conflict with others, infringes on rights of others, creates xenophobia and exhibit extreme characters of jingoism and chauvinism. The historian Lord Acton described nationalism as insanity, as early as in 1862. For Albert Einstein, "Nationalism is an infantile thing. It is the measles of mankind." George Orwell describes nationalism as, "the lunatic modern habit of identifying oneself with large power units and seeing everything in terms of competitive prestige."

The irrational passion of state called nationalism which purposely differentiated "we" from "others" has been the cause of almost all international wars including two world wars, civil wars and armed internal and religious conflicts in the history of the world. It was responsible for the racial extremism and The Holocaust of Hitler's Germany and many other violent dictatorial regimes. Even today, many armed conflicts are going on mostly in Africa and Middle East in the name of ethnicity, religion and religious sectarian divisions, with the latest manifestation of nationalism. Now, nationalism has evolved into neo-nationalism expressed with extreme populism. With its identity politics and extreme protectionism, the current populist ideologies continue to drive the people to craziness and consequent abnormal behaviour. This organic and evolving abnormal behaviour of state and its citizens in support of imaginary and artificially conceived notion of identifying a national identity and protecting and promoting its interests ignoring even the basic human rights of others is perceived as **'Behavioural Disorder'** of state.

COLONIALISM AND SPREAD OF THE CONCEPT OF NATION STATE

In addition to using nationalism to unify diverse people within their borders and strengthen the state system at home, European leaders also exported the nation-state system around the world during two waves of colonialism between 1500 and 1975. Colonialism is the effort by one country to establish settlements in a sparsely populated or uninhabited territory and to impose its political, economic, and cultural principles on that territory. The British had by far the largest colonial empire, followed by the French, the Netherlands, Belgium, Germany, and Italy. The colonizing powers met at the Berlin Conference in 1884–1885 and the European colonialism arbitrarily laid out the colonial map of Africa based on the limits of each colonizing power's influence in Africa and with no regard for the existing indigenous cultural or political arrangements. European colonies projected European power and the European approach to organizing space politically throughout the non-European world. It was through colonialism that the European concept of the nation-state became the model adopted around the world.

INHERITANCE OF DISORDERS BY YOUNG MODERN STATE SYSTEM

As discussed above, the concept of the nation-state and nationalism took hold in Europe in the nineteenth century and was exported around the world through European colonisation. Even so, the modern concept of state grew very slowly at first and has expanded rapidly only very recently. At the time of the Declaration of Independence by America in 1776, there were only some 35 empires, kingdoms, and countries in the entire world. By the beginning of the World War-II (WW-II), that number had only doubled to around 70. Following the WW-II, many former European colonies, finally achieved independence and consciously chose to retain their colonial borders, languages, and the very concept of statehood itself as a way of avoiding territorial and ethnic conflicts that might otherwise have torn these newly independent states apart. With the creation of these new independent countries, the number of states skyrocketed. In the forty years following 1945, some ninety African and Asian states were admitted to the United Nations. By 1990, there were 180 independent states and their number increased again following the disintegration in the 1990's of the USSR, Yugoslavia, and Czechoslovakia which created more than 20 new countries. With the admittance of South Sudan in July of 2011, the number of member states of the United Nations stands at 193 now. When compared to 5000 years old political history of mankind, 373 years old concept of "state" and 250 years old theory of "nation state", the present "modern nation state" system which is 75 years old is very young, as depicted in the following Table:

Timeline of creation of states

Timeline	Development
After treaties of Peace of Westphalia made in 1648	The Roman Empire state and its neighbouring states came into being in Europe, with demarcated territory and mutually recognized sovereign power, for the first time in history
After the French Revolution in 1789 (18th & 19th centuries)	Monarchy states were replaced with nation states conceived on the basis of shared religion, language, ethnicity, culture etc.,
At the end of World War-II & European colonialism and after formation of United Nations in 1945	The existing modern state system came into existence with 51 member states enrolled in the UN, initially.

Year	Number of member states in the UN
1950	60
1960	99
1970	127
1980	154
1990	159
2000	189
2011–2020	193*

*Holy See and State of Palestine are non-member observer states of the UN. There are other states like Taiwan, The Thomas Cook Islands etc which are not self-governing sovereign states.

Article 2 of the Charter of the UN, which prescribes the conditions for membership, has applied the principle of Westphalian independent sovereignty, when it says, "The Organization is based on the principle of the sovereign equality of all its Members", without making any reference to the political legitimacy of its member states. When Westphalian sovereignty laid down the foundation for independent state, nationalism was the driving force in the creation of many new states. Resultantly, the present modern nation state system is a mixture of independent sovereignty and the interventionist and imaginary nationalism. All modern states of today display the characters of both the Westphalian sovereign state and the nation state inherited from European political culture. Small and dependent states claim that they are sovereign and will not tolerate outside interference in their domestic affairs. Leaders of some strong states flex their muscles internationally in the name nationalism, claiming that the interest of their country is the first priority for them and they intrude in the domestic affairs of other states using force or otherwise on the pretext of safeguarding the interest of their nation. Neo-nationalist states are displaying their anti-liberal, anti-plural and protectionist behaviour in the name of national populism. Naturally, today many states are afflicted with congenital and behavioural disorders independently and jointly. The combined symptoms of congenital and behavioural disorders of state are apparently in display presently in about 45 - 55 fragile and conflict affected countries of the world.

3

MAJOR SUFFERINGS OF DISORDERS

CONGENITAL DISORDER LED TO BEHAVIOURAL DISORDER

Westphalian state system born with the congenital disorder (absence of mechanism to approve/generate political legitimacy) in mid-17th century innocuously led to its behavioural disorder in late 18th century in Europe with the introduction of a newly conceptualised political ideology of nationalism. Since the Westphalian state system provided unlimited power and authority within the state and international recognition with the new concept of sovereignty delinking Rome from state affairs, the monarch rulers of Europe felt reassured about their position, power and status and they established absolute monarchy regimes after becoming sovereign states.

This absolute monarchy led to misgovernance of King Louis XVI of France which triggered the French Revolution that began in 1789 and ended in the late 1790s with the ascent of Napoleon Bonaparte. During this period, French citizens razed and redesigned their country's political landscape, uprooting centuries-old institutions such as absolute monarchy and the feudal system. The upheaval was caused by widespread discontent with the French monarchy and the poor economic policies of King Louis XVI, who met his death by guillotine, as did his wife Marie Antoinette. Although it failed to achieve all of its goals and at times degenerated into a chaotic bloodbath, the French Revolution played a critical role in shaping modern nations by showing the world the power inherent in the will of the people. [1]

The French Revolution, in deed attempted to introduce an element of political legitimacy to the state by signifying the importance of citizens' approval to the government that was absent in monarchy rule. Napoleon's zeal to spread the maxim of French Revolution and in this process his attempt to expand the French rule to the entire Europe promoted the spirit of nationalism across every country of the Europe that made them to form their own nation state with each one's newly found unique identity. The elites who led the national movements impliedly got the approval of the people of their nationality to rule them (popular legitimacy) replacing monarchs. In result, the direction of the French Revolution to bring in some kind of political legitimacy to the state with people's participation by replacing monarchy and feudal system, got diverted to bring in an artificially created new political idea of nationalism. Instead of closing the crucial gap (state legitimacy) in the concept of Westphalian state system, the French Revolution introduced a new, irrational and emotive element (nationalism) in the system of state, making it more complicated. The present modern state system suffers from this crucial omission of state legitimacy as well as the mock idea of nationalism. Historically, these deficiencies have been taken advantage by the rulers, political parties, pressure groups, revolutionaries, non-state actors and terror groups to advance their vested interests. These negative elements of state system are expressed in the form of congenital and behavioural disorders of state and their manifestations impede the overall human development and further advancement of human civilization.

Had the Peace of Westphalia prescribed some kind of methodology either for the rulers to generate and demonstrate their political legitimacy or for the citizens to approve the authority of the government, the unrestrained misrule of monarchs would have been curtailed and the ideology of nationalism would not have been born as a result of the French Revolution to substitute state legitimacy, and consequently the political history and geography of the world would have been totally different since the end of the 18th century. May be, following the model of American Revolution and American state system, more sovereign states would have been created in Europe and the rest of the world on the then popular European political concepts like social contract, democracy, utilitarianism, liberalism, constitutionalism etc., in place of new found nationalism.

NATIONALISM AND LARGE-SCALE ARMED CONFLICTS

Since the seeds of nationalism were sown practically in the war fields of Europe, naturally the nationalism turned out to be the cause of almost all civil and international wars in 19th and 20th centuries and continues to be the cause for the ongoing civil wars and armed conflicts in many countries of Sub-Sharan Africa, South Asia and the Middle East.

As a political ideal, nationalism aspires to a congruence between state borders and the boundaries of the national community, so that the national group is contained in the territory of its state and the state contains only that nation. However, in reality, the borders of states and the boundaries of nations usually only partly overlap: not all residents of the state belong to the core national group (sometimes not even all citizens are part of the nation), and some members of the nation reside in other states. The lack of congruence between state and nation has given rise to several phenomena: wars that break out at approximately the time of nation-state formation; citizenship regimes that embrace co-national immigrants—i.e., immigrants belonging to the same nation—but exclude other immigrants; efforts by nation-states to nationalize additional territories and populations; and state policies that manage ethnic, religious, and national diversity within their borders.

A study done by the social scientists Andreas Wimmer and Brian Min in 2006 on "From Empire to Nation-State: Explaining Wars in the Modern World, 1816–2001", revealed that three types of wars were more prevalent at approximately the time of the foundation of nation-states: (1) wars of independence aiming to end foreign rule (e.g., the Algerian War of Independence in 1954–62 and the Kosovo conflict in 1998–99); (2) civil wars within new nation-states arising from struggles over the states' ethno-nationalist character, sometimes resulting in secessionist efforts by ethnic minorities (e.g., the 1963–67 uprising of the Somalian minority in Kenya, which demanded union of their area of residence with neighbouring Somalia); and (3) interstate wars declared by governments seeking to help oppressed co-nationals in new neighbouring nation-states (e.g., the Greco-Turkish war of 1921–22) and by new nation-states seeking to extend their rule to neighbouring territories inhabited by co-nationals (e.g., the German conquest of Alsace-Lorraine during the Franco-German War of 1871). [2]

According to this study, there were 484 distinct wars, including 77 wars of conquest, 111 inter-state wars, and 296 civil wars, 109 of which were secessionist and 187 non-secessionists. The dataset includes 156 territorial units, 140 of which were incorporated into an empire at some point (92 between 1816 and 2001), and 150 of which experienced nation-state creation. The thrust of the author's argument is that nationalism is a major force that has shaped world and domestic politics over the past 200 years, including many of the inter-state and civil wars fought during this period. In other words, the shift to nation-state is the major cause of war in the modern world. [3]

Today, leaders of the largest democracies of the world take pride in declaring themselves as staunch nationalists, their country is the greatest country in the world and for them their country is first. Their only assumption in making such statements is that people are unaware of the history of the world and particularly, the costly and dangerous implications of large-scale violence perpetrated on civilian public for the cause of nationalism and its huge impact on the world economy. It is too voluminous to cover the entire negative fallouts of nationalism from its birth in this chapter. Illustratively, let us see some of the world's most catastrophic and deadliest damages caused by nationalism in 20th century.

World War-I (1914–1918)

An ethnic nationalistic action triggered the world's first catastrophic war, the World War I fought between 1914 and 1918 in Europe. Archduke Franz Ferdinand, heir presumptive to the Austro-Hungarian Empire who visited the Bosnian capital, Sarajevo in 1914 was assassinated by Gavrilo Princip, a member of the Yugoslavist group Mlada Bosna. The political objective of the assassination was to break off Austria-Hungary's South Slav provinces, which Austria-Hungary had annexed from the Ottoman Empire, so that they could be combined into a Yugoslavia. During the conflict, Germany, Austria-Hungary, Bulgaria and the Ottoman Empire (the Central Powers) fought against Great Britain, France, Russia, Italy, Romania, Japan and the United States (the Allied Powers). Thanks to the new military technologies and the horrors of trench warfare, World War I saw unprecedented levels of slaughter, carnage and destruction. It is also one of the deadliest conflicts in history, with an estimated 9 million combatant deaths and 13 million civilian deaths as a direct result of the war, resulting in genocides, and the related 1918 influenza pandemic caused another 17–100 million deaths worldwide. Finally, Allied Powers claimed victory. The First World War destroyed empires, created numerous new nation-states, encouraged independence movements in Europe's colonies, pushed the United States to become a world power and led directly to Soviet communism and the rise of Hitler. The irony is that the reaction among the people in Austria, however, was mild, almost indifferent to the news of the assassination of the heir presumptive to the Austro-Hungarian Empire. Nevertheless, the political effect of the murder of the heir to the throne was significant that triggered nationalistic sentiments and a massive and catastrophic world war. This was nothing but the madness of nationalism.

World War-II (1939–1945)

The spark of fire ignited by nationalism in World War I was failed to be extinguished for two decades and again a still larger fire broke out in 1939 in the next edition, World War II. The major cause for the World War II was the loss and humiliation meted out to Germany in World War I, the following Treaty of Versailles and consequent rise of Nazism by Hitler to take revenge on Allied Powers. The death and destruction of World War I was so horrible that it was called "the war to end all wars." Yet, the agreement to end World War I did not resolve the problems of the world and, according to some historians, lead directly to the next catastrophe: World War II. Despite strong pacifist sentiment after World War I, its aftermath still caused irredentist and revanchist nationalism in several European states. These sentiments were especially marked in Germany because of the significant territorial, colonial, and financial losses incurred by the Treaty of Versailles signed at the end of the World War I. The immediate precipitating event was the invasion of Poland by Nazi Germany on September 1, 1939, and the subsequent declaration of war on Germany made by Britain and France, but many other prior events have been suggested as ultimate causes. Primary themes in historical analysis of the war's origins include the political takeover of Germany in 1933 by Adolf Hitler and the Nazi Party; Japanese militarism against China; Italian aggression against Ethiopia; and Germany's initial success in negotiating a neutrality pact with the Soviet Union to divide territorial control of Eastern Europe between them. All these events were driven by the nationalist compulsions of the respective states.

The principal belligerents were the Axis powers—Germany, Italy, and Japan—and the Allies—France, Great Britain, the United States, the Soviet Union, and, to a lesser extent, China. The war came to an end by the American's atomic bombing of Hiroshima and Nagasaki of Japan in August 1945 and the Allied powers won the war.

The behavioural disorder of nationalism touched its peak of insanity with new dimensions in the World War II and caused unprecedented and unimaginable damages to the human race. World War II was the deadliest military conflict in history. Atom bomb was used for the first and last time in WW II. The United States detonated two atomic bombs over the Japanese cities of Hiroshima and Nagasaki in August 1945, killing 210,000 people—children, women, and men. An estimated total of 70–85 million people perished, which was about 3% of the 1940 world population (est. 2.3 billion). Deaths directly caused by the war (including military and civilians' fatalities) are estimated at 50–56 million, with an additional estimated 19 to 28 million deaths from war-related disease and famine. Recent historical scholarship has shed new light on the topic of the Second World War casualties. Research in Russia since the collapse of the Soviet Union has caused a revision of estimates of Soviet WW II fatalities. According to Russian government figures, the USSR's loss within post-war borders now stands at 26.6 million, including 8 to 9 million due to famine and disease. In August 2009 the Polish Institute of National Remembrance (IPN) researchers estimated Poland's dead at between 5.6 and 5.8 million. Historian Rüdiger Overmans of the Military History Research Office (Germany) published a study in 2000 that estimated the German military dead and missing at 5.3 million, including 900,000 men conscripted from outside of Germany's 1937 borders, in Austria, and in east-central Europe. The People's Republic of China puts its war dead at 20 million, while the Japanese government puts its casualties due to the war at 3.1 million.

Post-war impact was also serious. Six years of ground battles and bombing resulted in widespread destruction of homes and physical capital. Discrimination and persecution were widespread, with the Holocaust as the most horrific example. Many people were forced to give up or abandon their property and periods of hunger became common, even in the relatively prosperous Western Europe. Families were separated for long periods of time, and many children lost their fathers and witnessed the horrors of battle. The study found that living in a war-torn country during World War II was consistently associated with having poorer health later in life. In addition, people exposed to the war had lower education levels as adults, took more years to acquire that education, were less likely to marry, and were less satisfied with their lives as older adults. [4]

Hitler's Nazism & The Holocaust

Hitler's Nazism or Social Nationalism degenerated the newly emerged political idea of nationalism to its worst expression, leaving its impact internationally (WW II) as well as locally (The Holocaust), which still remains the darkest period in the entire history of human civilization. In its intense nationalism, mass appeal, and dictatorial rule, Nazism shared many elements with Italian fascism. However, Nazism was far more extreme both in its ideas and practice. In almost every respect it was an anti-intellectual and atheoretical movement, emphasizing the will of the charismatic dictator as the sole source of inspiration of a people and a nation, as well as a vision of annihilation of all enemies of the Aryan Volk as the one and only goal of Nazi policy. The Nazis' ideology rested on several key ideas, such as nationalism, racial superiority (eugenics), antisemitism, and anticommunism. The crimes that Nazis committed were linked to a system of belief and a set of practices.

Nazi ideology was synonymous with Hitler's worldview. According to this there was no equality between people, but only a racial hierarchy. In this view blond, blue-eyed, Nordic German Aryans were at the top, while Jews were located at the lowest rung. They came to be regarded as an anti-race, the arch-enemies of the Aryans. All other coloured people were placed in between depending upon their external features. Once in power, the Nazis quickly began to implement their dream of creating an exclusive racial community of pure Germans by physically eliminating all those who were seen as 'undesirable' in the extended empire. Nazis wanted only a society of 'pure and healthy Nordic Aryans'. They alone were considered 'desirable'. Only they were seen as worthy of prospering and multiplying against all others who were classed as 'undesirable'. This meant that even those Germans who were seen as impure or abnormal had no right to exist.

Hitler's ideology grew out of his fantasy of the German nation as an actual organism, or body (politic). "Our movement alone," Hitler declared, "was capable of creating a national organism." In place of the State, Hitler said, must be set "the living organism—the people." Hitler conceived of Germany as a body politic consisting of German people as its cells. It followed that the purpose of politics was to preserve the body politic: to "maintain the substance of the people in bodily and mental health, in good order and purity." According to Hitler, the supreme test of every political institution was: "Does it serve to preserve the people or not."

The National Socialistic movement was based upon an ideology that was a subset of the ideology of nationalism. Nazism represented a frenzy of nationalistic hysteria. Jane Roberts states that Hitler brought to flower all of the "most morbid nationalistic fantasies" that had been growing for centuries. The grandiose celebration of a nation's "inalienable right to seek domination," she says, focused finally in Hitler's Germany. Nazism enacted the deepest, and darkest dreams contained within the ideology of nationalism.

When Hitler and the Nazis came to power in 1933, they instituted a series of measures aimed at persecuting Germany's Jewish citizens. By late 1938, Jews were banned from most public places in Germany. During the war, the Nazis' anti-Jewish campaigns increased in scale and ferocity. In the invasion and occupation of Poland, German troops shot thousands of Polish Jews, confined many to ghettoes where they starved to death and began sending others to death camps in various parts of Poland, where they were either killed immediately or forced into slave labour. In 1941, when Germany invaded the Soviet Union, Nazi death squads machine-gunned tens of thousands of Jews in the western regions of Soviet Russia. In early 1942, at the Wannsee Conference near Berlin, the Nazi Party decided on the last phase of what it called the "Final Solution" of the "Jewish problem" and spelled out plans for the systematic murder of all European Jews in the Holocaust. In 1942 and 1943, Jews in the western occupied countries including France and Belgium were deported by the thousands to the death camps mushrooming across Europe. In Poland, huge death camps such as Auschwitz began operating with ruthless efficiency. The murder of Jews in German-occupied lands stopped only in the last months of the war, as the German armies were retreating toward Berlin. By the time Hitler committed suicide in April 1945, some 6 million Jews were killed. [5]

This cruel, brutal, barbaric and extremely abnormal behaviour of Hitler in the name of racial nationalism was totally against the civilization progressed in Europe in the period of Renaissance and Enlightenment. It is the superlative example for the negative fallout of hyper-nationalism and behavioural disorder of state. It demonstrated to the world to which extent the ideal of nationalism can be extended to make one person's idiotic fantasies and dreams come into reality, even by murdering millions of fellow citizens. This kind of misinterpretation and misapplication of the concept of nationalism in any other manner for any other purpose is always possible. Right now, religious, sectarian and ethical nationalism are cause for armed conflicts in many countries. North Korea and some right-wing populist states are moving towards the direction of facism. The concept of purity of race followed by Hitler is applied at present to purify religion (purification of Islam by fundamentalists and elimination of Rohingya Muslims in Myanmar) and eliminate religion from atheist society (genocide of Uighur Muslims in China). After Hitler's disastrous Holocaust, ideally the imaginary and dangerous notion of nationalism should have gained notoriety in politics and it should have been totally abandoned from the political theory and practice for good. Unfortunately, it did not happen. On the other hand, it gained more approval and application in the formation of new states after the end of WW II and colonialism, worldwide. Presently, in response to the changing socio-economic conditions, the classic idea of nationalism has mutated into neo-nationalism or national populism.

Ethnic Yugoslav Wars (1991–1999)

Another major conflict broke out on the ground of ethnic nationalism in Yugoslavia at the end of the last century, during which period many countries joined the bandwagon of economic liberalisation and globalization and begin to enjoy the economic success. The former Yugoslavia was a Socialist state created after the German occupation in World War II and a bitter civil war. A federation of six republics, it brought together Serbs, Croats, Bosnian Muslims, Albanians, Slovenes and others under a comparatively relaxed communist regime. Tensions between these groups were successfully suppressed under the leadership of President Tito. After Tito's death in 1980, tensions re-emerged. Calls for more autonomy within Yugoslavia by nationalist groups led in 1991 to declarations of independence in Croatia and Slovenia. The Serb-dominated Yugoslav army lashed out, first in Slovenia and then in Croatia. Thousands were killed in the later conflict which was paused in 1992 under a UN-monitored ceasefire. Bosnia, with a complex mix of Serbs, Muslims and Croats, was next to try for independence. Bosnia's Serbs, backed by Serbs elsewhere in Yugoslavia, resisted. Under leader Radovan Karadzic, they threatened bloodshed if Bosnia's Muslims and Croats - who outnumbered Serbs - broke away. Despite European blessing for the move in a 1992 referendum, war came fast. Yugoslav army units, withdrawn from Croatia and renamed the Bosnian Serb Army, carved out a huge swathe of Serb-dominated territory. Over a million Bosnian Muslims and Croats were driven out from their homes in ethnic cleansing. Serbs too suffered. The capital Sarajevo was besieged and shelled. UN peacekeepers brought in to quell the fighting, were seen ineffective. International peace efforts to stop the war failed, the UN was humiliated and over 100,000 died. The war ended in 1995 after the NATO bombed the Bosnian Serbs and Muslim and Croat armies made gains on the ground. A US-brokered peace divided Bosnia into two self-governing entities, a Bosnian Serb republic, and a Muslim-Croat federation lightly bound by a central government. In August 1995, the Croatian army stormed areas in Croatia under Serb control prompting thousands to flee.

Soon Croatia and Bosnia were fully independent. Slovenia and Macedonia had already gone. Montenegro left later. In 1999, Kosovo's ethnic Albanians fought Serbs in another brutal war to gain independence. Serbia ended the conflict beaten, battered and alone. [6]

Indeed, for sheer horror, especially for the savagery of crimes against non-combatants, the only apt comparison with the Yugoslav conflict is World War II itself. The similarity is not coincidental: many of the murderous hatreds that burned like an acid through the territory of the former Yugoslavia during the four-plus years from June 1991 through November 1995 had their origins in the same ideological-cum-religious-cum-ethnic conflicts that made the Balkans a killing field half a century before. The human toll of the recent conflict, like that of the earlier one, is mind-numbingly large. As many as 300,000 persons may have lost their lives since 1991—many of them wilfully slaughtered, others the victims of starvation, disease, or exposure. And as many as two million persons may have been forcibly displaced from their homes or have otherwise become refugees. [7]

Rwandan Genocide

The Rwandan genocide, also known as the genocide against the Tutsi is a gruesome illustration of violence due to ethnic rivalries to catch power in a state. It was a mass slaughter of Tutsi, Twa, and moderate Hutu in Rwanda, which took place between 7 April and 15 July 1994 during the Rwandan Civil War.

In 1990, the Rwandan Patriotic Front (RPF), a rebel group composed of Tutsi refugees, invaded northern Rwanda from their base in Uganda, initiating the Rwandan Civil War. Neither side was able to gain a decisive advantage in the war, and the Rwandan government led by President Juvénal Habyarimana signed the Arusha Accords with the RPF on 4 August 1993. Many historians argue that a genocide against the Tutsi had been planned for at least a year. However, Habyarimana's assassination on 6 April 1994 created a power vacuum and ended peace accords. Genocidal killings began the following day when soldiers, police, and militia executed key Tutsi and moderate Hutu military and political leaders.

The scale and brutality of the massacre caused shock worldwide, but no country intervened to forcefully stop the killings. Most of the victims were killed in their own villages or towns, many by their neighbours and fellow villagers. Hutu gangs searched out victims hiding in churches and school buildings. The militia murdered victims with machetes and rifles. An estimated 500,000 to 1,000,000 Rwandans were killed, about 70% of the country's Tutsi population. Sexual violence was rife, with an estimated 250,000 to 500,000 women raped during the genocide. The RPF quickly resumed the civil war once the genocide started and captured all government territory, ending the genocide and forcing the government and genocidaires into Zaire. The genocide had lasting and profound effects on Rwanda and neighbouring countries. In 1996, the RPF-led Rwandan government launched an offensive into Zaire (now the Democratic Republic of the Congo), home to the exiled leaders of the former Rwandan government and many Hutu refugees, starting the First Congo War and killing an estimated 200,000 people. [8]

COMBINED EFFECTS OF DISORDERS

At the beginning of this chapter, we noted that the congenital disorder of state led to its behavioural disorder. Since lack of state legitimacy was substituted with nationalistic ideologies to attract public and get their approval for governance, nationalism captured the centre-stage of national and international political sphere and hence its impact on the political history of the world in the 19th and 20th century was very significant. Consequently, the symptoms of both the disorders overlapped one another. Today, many fragile and conflict affected countries are afflicted with both the disorders, reinforcing and complementing each other. Whenever a government suspects its political legitimacy, it invokes the magic of nationalism to gain the support of a majority section of people, based on certain currently appealing grounds in order to claim implied legitimacy.

On the contrary, in a few countries, nationalism is promoted intentionally by a group of people taking advantage of some past and forgotten ethnic or religious rivalries to gain the support of a group of people (legitimacy) and capture power even by violent means. But such violent conflicts continue to persists even after the formation of government by that group which make the government weak and illegitimate. Such states are also termed as fragile and conflict affected states.

Appreciating the problems of such weak states and their consequential effect on human development, Professor Robert Irwin Rotberg states that nation-states fail because they are convulsed by internal violence and can no longer deliver positive political goods to their inhabitants. Their governments lose legitimacy, and the very nature of the particular nation-state itself becomes illegitimate in the eyes and in the hearts of a growing plurality of its citizens. The rise and fall of nation-states is not new, but in a modern era when national states constitute the building blocks of a legitimate world order the violent disintegration and palpable weakness of selected African, Asian, Oceanic, and Latin American states threaten the very foundation of that system. International organizations and big powers consequently find themselves sucked disconcertingly into a maelstrom of anomic internal conflict and messy humanitarian relief. Desirable international norms such as stability and predictability thus become difficult to achieve when so many of the globe's newer nation-states waver precariously between weakness and failure, with some truly failing, or even collapsing. In a time of terror, moreover, appreciating the nature of and responding to the dynamics of nation-state failure have become central to critical policy debates. How best to strengthen weak states and prevent state failure are among the urgent questions of the twenty-first century. [9]

The Armed Conflict Location & Event Data Project (ACLED) after studying the conflicts that took place in 2019 enumerated 10 conflicts to worry about in 2020 with facts and figures. This report confirms the premise that congenital and behavioural disorders of state are responsible for the increasing internal conflicts. The report states that in 2019, the world witnessed a drastic increase in violent disorder that assumed many forms: protests from Lebanon to Hong Kong and Iraq to Chile; geopolitical competition in Yemen and Syria; dominant insurgencies in Somalia and Afghanistan; a cartel-insurgency in Mexico; and a diffuse, adaptable militant threat across the Sahel. Two problems immediately stand out: the world is significantly more violent now than a decade ago, and today's conflict forms are strongly localized — types of violence, agents, targets, and solutions are unique to their local context. This is partially because governments in the world's most violent places are no longer in control of their territories, nor show any interest or ability to resume control through direct or indirect authority. Governments are also much more likely to use violence against their citizens without international reproach. The rise of authoritarianism (nationalism) and impunity (lack of legitimacy) — has generated significant public reaction in the form of mass protest movements, but it has also increased the level of violence imposed upon civilians and political competition. [10]

To get a picture of the state of affairs of the countries afflicted with congenital as well as behavioural disorders, let us study the present political and socio-economic conditions of some of the Sub-Saharan and Middle East countries and the ongoing Syrian armed conflict.

Sub-Saharan Armed Conflicts

Recent studies show that most of the Sub-Saharan countries are at the bottom of the ranking list of fragile and conflict afflicted states. A World Bank report dated Apr 23, 2020 states that several long-standing challenges remain and are holding back progress in Sub-Saharan Africa. Around 640 million people currently live without electricity in Africa – 210 million of which are in fragile and conflict-affected countries. Public debt levels and debt risk are rising, which might jeopardize debt sustainability in some countries; the availability of good jobs has not kept pace with the number of entrants in the labour force; fragility is costing the subcontinent a half of a percentage point of growth per year; and gender gaps persist and are keeping the continent from reaching its full growth and innovation potential. More than 416 million Africans still live in extreme poverty.

Prof. Dr. Matthias Basedau, Director of the GIGA Institute for African Affairs analyses the real nature, causes and impact of conflicts in Sub-Saharan countries as follows: Religious violence has apparently become a widespread phenomenon in sub-Saharan Africa. Obviously, the problem is substantial and has the potential to grow. Regarding interreligious conflicts, countries with mixed religious populations in coastal countries in West and East Africa are at risk of an escalation into violence, as has been the case in Ethiopia, Côte d'Ivoire, Sudan, and the Central African Republic. The geographical hotspots of theological armed conflicts are the Sahel, specifically Mali, Nigeria, and Somalia. The Islamist rebels in these countries have ties with global groups like al-Qaida and the Islamic State (IS). Although Islamists have been weakened in Mali and Nigeria in recent years and months, these conflicts have spilled over into neighbouring countries. The Sahel region as a whole is constantly under threat: Nigeria's Boko Haram (officially called Jama'atu Ahlis Sunna Lidda'awati wal-Jihad) has staged attacks in Cameroon, Chad, and Niger, while terrorists tied to the Somali group Al-Shabaab have attacked civilian targets in Kenya and Uganda. This violence has resulted in substantial bloodshed. According to the Uppsala Conflict Data Program (UCDP), the conflict in Nigeria involving Boko Haram has claimed the lives of more than 20,000 people since 2009. In Somalia, more than 30,000 have perished since the early 1990s. The number of people killed in clashes between Muslim herders and Christian farmers in Nigeria's middle belt exceeds 10,000. Thousands have also been killed in the Central African Republic (CAR). These numbers only include direct battle-related deaths and not indirect deaths that result from worsened living conditions. Millions have become internally displaced persons (IDPs) or have fled to neighbouring or Western countries because of these conflicts. Violent conflict – whether religious or not – always severely hinders sound economic, political, and social development.

Often, religious and ethnic differences run parallel in countries with diverse populations like the CAR and Nigeria. Such identity overlaps have proved to be a determinant of religious and other armed conflicts (Basedau, Pfeiffer, and Vüllers 2016), especially when combined with feelings of marginalisation. The effects of weak states and poor governance also contribute to such conflicts. The lack of social and economic development and corrupt politicians in various countries make parts of their populations vulnerable to radical ideology – which seems to be an alternative to secular governments that fail to deliver. Unemployed young men without perspectives are particularly vulnerable to being recruited, as they have little to lose when joining a rebel group. A weak state can also give rise to religious conflicts besides the direct motivations by potential religious rebels. Uncontrolled areas in the Sahel, the Horn of Africa, and Nigeria enable rebels to operate and to withdraw. Furthermore, weak security forces either are unable to contain rebellions or engage in indiscriminate responses that push many civilian bystanders into the arms of religious extremists. For example, the original leader of Boko Haram was apparently assassinated while in the custody of the Nigerian police, turning him into a martyr. International efforts to battle extremists might also have adverse effects. Terrorist attacks in Kenya, Uganda, and Western countries seem to be acts of revenge for military involvement in the fight against Islamist groups. Nevertheless, Malians overwhelmingly welcomed the 2013 French-led intervention that pushed back the Islamist rebels who had occupied the northern part of the country.

Some scholars go as far as to completely deny any role of religion (see, for instance, Hasenclever and Sändig 2014). According to their arguments, rebels who use religion in their claims are merely instrumentalising religion or espousing shallow rhetoric. It is true that religious ideas and religious identities can be a powerful source of mobilisation; however, that does not convincingly exclude religion as part of the causal logic – especially in the deeply religious region of sub-Saharan Africa. This school of thought cannot rule out the fact that leaders are true believers and does not explain a range of behaviour – for instance, religious extremists dehumanising those they attack as "infidels" and "apostates" or killing themselves in suicide bombings. Islamists in Mali, Somalia, and Nigeria also imposed religious laws in the territories they controlled. Non-religious causes cannot explain all these kinds of behaviour – particular religious convictions can.

Instrumentalization does in fact confirm the role of religion in the causal logic. Those who cynically instrumentalise, be they leaders or "false prophets," need their supporters and foot soldiers to believe in their religious motivations. Discussing instrumentalization rather points to the fact that religious and non-religious factors mix. Mundane factors such as weak states, insufficient government, and international responses make states vulnerable to rebellion and insurgency, identity-based grievances of religious groups, and religious ideologies. Sometimes, outside support from religious extremists can add fuel to the fire and facilitate mobilisation, radicalisation, and gruesome violence. It is more likely that the combination of religious and non-religious factors explains the emergence, duration, and intensity of religious armed conflicts and other forms of religious violence. [11] The above findings of the study also apply to the North African countries, Sudan and Libya where armed conflicts continue to take place.

Armed Conflicts of the Middle East

Author Bettina Koch in her article "Unmasking 'Religious' Conflicts and Religious Radicalisation in the Middle East" has exposed the weakness of pseudo nationalism with religious and sectarian elements that contribute armed conflicts in the Middle East, with historical narratives. She writes that for conflicts geographically situated in the Middle East, the tendency of labelling a conflict 'sectarian' or 'religious' is particularly common. Yet, ignoring other possible root causes undermines the possibility for conflict resolution. If one concerns oneself with conflicts in the Middle East, then the focus lies instantly on the religion(s) of Islam, Shia-Sunni conflicts, and the concept of jihad. Yet, as Michael Bonner (2006, 120) notes, even the great fitna, the strife in the Muslim community after the third calif's death, was fought 'over leadership, morality, and the allocation of resources.' Bonner's observation suggests we be cautious when interpreting inter-communal conflict as religious right from the beginning of the history of Islam. If one looks at two of the most prominent conflicts, the Iranian Revolution and the still ongoing conflict between Israel and Palestine, one may observe another phenomenon, namely the phenomenon of religious reinterpretation that also displays internal tensions between conservative and progressive forces. Israel – Palestine conflict rose from territorial dispute. The process of reinterpreting a conflict in religious terms that goes hand in hand with religious radicalisations is perhaps even more visible in the Iranian Revolution. As Morteza Motahari (1985, 208), the chief-ideologue of the Iranian Revolution has put it, Khomeini 'fought against oppression, injustice, colonialism and exploitation'. These issues can be read in religious as well as secular terms. Prior to the revolution, Khomeini consistently translated his message to the general public into secular language. If one keeps in mind what actually sparked the conflict in Syria, one may instantly have some doubts about narratives that picture the conflict in Syria as just another sectarian or religious conflict. At the beginning, this was certainly not the case. Yet, reframing the narrative of the conflict instantly took place. The regime promptly accused the opposition of being sectarian Islamists. Eventually, each group accused each other of pursuing sectarian goals. The question is, of course, not only who is fighting whom, but also, and more importantly, for what reason. Moreover, it is also important to notice which external forces are supporting whom and what is the rationale behind it.

After brilliantly analysing the narratives of Middle East conflicts, the author concludes that conflicts, however, are not always what they are, but also, transforming narratives about them may change perception of the conflict entirely. Yet, a changing narrative does not necessarily mean that a conflict's root causes have disappeared. They are only harder to identify. While one can already observe in older conflicts the power of reinterpretation that, in tendency, favours religious over secular readings, current conflicts, like the ones in Syria and Iraq, in particular are marked by another dimension; namely, existing power vacuums that allow sectarian non-state movements to engage in the conflict and to attract a significant amount of media attention – with a tendency of blowing their significance out of proportion. While in the conflicts narrated above some sectarian elements certainly exist, their role is at best part of the conflict, and sectarian issues usually do not belong to any of the current conflicts' root causes. Thus, in most cases, it is more appropriate to speak at best of partial sectarian conflicts or of conflicts that are partially (ab)used for sectarian goals. Yet, can we speak about a religious conflict if a party that was not present initially tries to use it for its sectarian goals that are unrelated to the conflict's original causes? [12]

Syrian Conflicts

Syria is the best place in the world to witness the mutually reinforcing multidimensional effects of weak state legitimacy and madness of nationalism based on religious sectarian and ethnic divisions. It is also the country which explicitly demonstrates to the world that just remaining in power would authorise the rulers to kill their own civilian citizens in a massive scale with their military power as well as with help of the forces of other nations.

Even before the conflict began, many Syrians were complaining about high unemployment, corruption and a lack of political freedom under President Bashar al-Assad, who succeeded his father, Hafez, after he died in 2000. In March 2011, pro-democracy demonstrations erupted in the southern city of Deraa, inspired by the "Arab Spring" in neighbouring countries. When the government used deadly force to crush the dissent, protests demanding the president's resignation erupted nationwide. The unrest spread and the crackdown intensified. Opposition supporters took up arms, first to defend themselves and later to rid their areas of security forces. Mr Assad vowed to crush what he called "foreign-backed terrorism".

The violence rapidly escalated and the country descended into civil war. It is now more than a battle between those who are for or against Mr Assad. Many groups and countries - each with their own agendas - are involved, making the situation far more complex and prolonging the fighting. They have been accused of fostering hatred between Syria's religious groups, pitching the Sunni Muslim majority against the president's Shia Alawite sect. Such divisions have led both sides to commit atrocities, torn communities apart and dimmed hopes of peace. They have also allowed the jihadist groups Islamic State (IS) and al-Qaeda to flourish. Syria's Kurds, who want the right of self-government but have not fought Mr Assad's forces, have added another dimension to the conflict. The government's key supporters have been Russia and Iran, while Turkey, Western powers and several Gulf Arab states have backed the opposition.

The Syrian Observatory for Human Rights, a UK-based monitoring group with a network of sources on the ground, had documented the deaths of 367,965 people by December 2018. The figure did not include 192,035 people who it said were missing and presumed dead. Meanwhile, the Violations Documentation Center, which relies on activists inside Syria, has recorded what it considers violations of international humanitarian law and human rights law, including attacks on civilians. It had documented 191,219 battle-related deaths, including 123,279 civilians, as of December 2018. Besides causing hundreds of thousands of deaths, the war has left 1.5 million people with permanent disabilities, including 86,000 who have lost limbs. More than half of the Syrians have been displaced since 2011. At least 6.2 million Syrians are internally displaced, while another 5.7 million have fled abroad. Neighbouring Lebanon, Jordan and Turkey, which are hosting 93% of them, have struggled to cope with one of the largest refugee exoduses in recent history. By February 2019, some 13 million people were estimated to be in need of humanitarian assistance, including 5.2 million in acute need. The warring parties have made the problems worse by refusing aid agencies' access to many of those in need. Some 1.1 million people were living in hard-to-reach areas as of February 2019. Much of

Syria's rich cultural heritage has also been destroyed. All the six of the country's Unesco World Heritage sites have been damaged significantly. Entire neighbourhoods have been levelled across the country. [13]

In 2019, the Amnesty International reported that the government and the allied forces continued to commit war crimes and other serious violations of international humanitarian law, including indiscriminate direct attacks on civilians and civilian objects. Government forces, with the support of Russia, repeatedly attacked Idlib and Hama governorates in north-western Syria and the northern part of Aleppo governorate, all of which were controlled by Hay'at Tahrir al-Sham. They carried out attacks on civilian homes, schools, bakeries, rescue operations, hospitals and medical facilities, by artillery shelling and air strikes, killing and injuring hundreds of civilians, including rescue and medical workers. Between April and September, at least 51 medical facilities and 59 schools were damaged as a result of hostilities in Idlib, Hama and northern Aleppo, according to the UN Office for the Coordination of Humanitarian Affairs (OCHA). [14]

NEED FOR STANDARDIZATION AND VALIDATION OF STATE

Surprisingly, the above noted countries and many other states like North Korea, Afghanistan, and Myanmar having similar conditions of various degrees continue to function as sovereign states recognized by the UN and international community. Under which authority do they rule these countries? Under what right they kill and torture their own citizens? In which authority they deny the basic human rights of their citizens? Why does the international community recognize them as sovereign states? Under which international authority other nations send their forces to kill the civilian citizens of these states? The physical weakness and mental imbalance of these states caused by the congenital and behavioural disorders is the only answer to all these and other related questions. In this healthy and mature world order there cannot be any rational and acceptable answers to these questions except the above one. In the present multipolar competitive world, big powers like the USA, China and Russia and their proxy states take advantage of the situations of these weak states to advance their geo-political and economic interests. Around 50 states in the world are not only suffering from the congenital and behavioural disorders, but also exposed easily to the above dangerous viruses from big powers. In this age of globalization, every product and service delivered to the public is standardized and validated for the safe and easy use by consumers across the world. The constitution and the functional process of the world's most powerful political unit called state, which exercises unlimited and unquestionable control and authority over its citizens is yet to be standardized and validated with reference to its political legitimacy and behaviour, for the benefit of its own citizens and the international community.

4

COMPREHENSIVE AND SELF-ENFORCEABLE STATE LEGITIMACY

STATE LEGITIMACY AND HUMAN DEVELOPMENT

Earmarked territory, population living in such a territory, government and sovereignty are considered the essential elements of a state. Except the government, all other three elements are not qualifying in nature and need no validation. However, the government, whatever be its form, needs the approval of majority of the citizens enabling it to enforce its laws and ensure order in the state. This approval is called state legitimacy. This essential element of state legitimacy was failed to be incorporated directly or indirectly at the time of the birth of Westphalian state system in 1648 that we follow even now. This discrepancy is construed as congenital disorder of the state. Yet modern nation states, either formed centuries ago or created in the last decade, democratic or authoritarian, all of them now claim political legitimacy in some or other form to enable to exercise their sovereign power. This so claimed political legitimacy exists in different countries in different norms (from single party rule to theocracy) that survives in various degree of approval (from full democracy to authoritarian) and with different measures of functional efficiency (from

Finland to Afghanistan). The UN and the world community of states recognize all such states without going into the correctness of their claims. Then, where is the need to rectify this disorder now?

Though state legitimacy is a political concept, its importance is viewed with various dimensions. Since our focus is mainly on major global risks and the human development, let us restrict our discussion relevant to these points only. State plays the key role in addressing the important global risks of climate change, poverty, inequality and armed conflicts. A government which enjoys strong approval and support of the public can only address these crucial issues effectively and improve the quality of life of their citizens to a global average standard. If a government succeeds in these efforts, its strength of legitimacy will grow automatically and it will continue to remain in power, notwithstanding its current status of legitimacy and legacy. China, Saudi Arabia and the UAE are the latest example for this. If a government lacking in legitimacy attempts to rule by coercion or creating illusions, its primary challenge would be to remain in power as long as possible and therefore the global risks and the human development would get the least attention of such government. The human development conditions deteriorate, as the state legitimacy weakens. Fragile and conflict affected sub-Saharan countries, Afghanistan, North Korea, Haiti, Yemen and Venezuela are illustrating the above facts currently.

States are legitimate when citizens accept their right to rule over them. But legitimacy is also a political process of bringing order to social relations, and political actors are often central to it. Legitimacy matters because without it there is likely to be conflict and disorder. All states need a degree of legitimacy to govern effectively. Understanding when citizens are likely to confer or withdraw state legitimacy requires investigating social norms. The depth and durability of a state's legitimacy has direct effects on the feasibility of development processes, and on the effectiveness of external efforts to support them. [1]

State legitimacy is a key aspect of state-society relations. State repression and violence, which occur in many conflict-affected contexts, result in negative experiences of citizens with the state, a legacy of mistrust, and rejection of the legitimacy of state institutions. In situations of fragility, the inability or unwillingness of states to provide for the welfare of citizens and to improve standards of living has also undermined trust between the state and society. The development of state capacity to manage competing interests and to be responsive to citizen's needs thus has the potential to improve legitimacy. [2]

STATE LEGITIMACY – KEY TO HUMAN DEVELOPMENT

The legitimacy is not a static feature in the governance of a state as its value keeps changing mainly depending on the degree of efficiency of its service delivery system (outputs). Legitimacy is the most essential organic element of the state machinery without which it would become dysfunctional. Depending on the degree of malfunction of states, they are called as weak or quasi or failed or collapsed states. In general, they are also termed as fragile and conflict affected states. The nature of such classified states, their politico-economic-social conditions and functional efficiency have been studied a lot. In these studies, among other indicators, lack of political legitimacy of the rulers is enumerated as one of the conditions of such states. But these studies failed to appreciate the fact that except the weak legitimacy, all other attributes and conditions of such dysfunctional states reflect the performance of the government, whereas, the state legitimacy is the engine driving the organic functioning of the government. Legitimacy is the fundamental and legal requirement of a government and it indicates its credibility and capability in securing the safety of the public and delivery of essential public goods and services to its citizens. If there exists a reasonably legitimate government, such government can manage to maintain peace, order and stability in the state and always strive for the overall development of its citizens, with internal and/or external resources. Except in cases of unmanageable natural disasters or strong external interventions to destabilise the government, a legitimate government would not fail from its fundamental duties of safeguarding the essential interests of the public. In other words, political legitimacy of a government is the source for good governance. If the source is strong and stable, the outputs from the government will satisfy the expectations of its citizens and if it is weak, then there will be inefficient and insufficient outcomes. Political legitimacy is the key driver of state functions and its weakness can be the main and the only cause for making a state fragile and dysfunctional. Therefore, weak legitimacy is not one of the symptoms of a dysfunctional state as claimed by various studies; on the other hand, it is the source of the state's fragile conditions, which leads to the poor performance of the government contributing to other indicators of dysfunctional state. This fact can easily be verified in the present status of fragile and conflict affected countries.

So called 'fragile states' and how best to engage with them have emerged as a key priority in the international development community. This concern has surfaced from the confluence of several factors, including (i) an emphasis on human security and peacebuilding; (ii) a concern with the relationship between state effectiveness and development; and (iii) a belief that underdevelopment and insecurity (individual and international) are related. One billion people, including about 340m of the world's extreme poor, are estimated to live in this group of between 30–50 'fragile' countries, located mainly in Africa, that are 'falling behind and falling apart' (Collier, 2007). There is now consensus that without a strengthened model of international engagement, these countries will continue to fall behind. It is recognised that delivering aid in these contexts cannot be 'business as usual', and that fragile situations require a co-ordinated, cross-sectoral approach that combines support to state-building and peacebuilding and uses whole-of-government approaches. But fragile states are 'under-aided', even against allocation models that take their performance into account. Aid flows are excessively volatile, poorly coordinated, and often reactive rather than preventive. The fragile states' agenda is surrounded by a great deal of critical debate. The term itself is highly contested –some argue it implicitly contains normative assumptions of how states should perform and a misguided notion that all states will eventually converge around a Western model of statehood. But in spite of the many criticisms of how fragile states have been conceptualised, few would dispute the severe impacts this group of states impose on the security and well-being of their populations. [3]

World Bank 2007 report points out that fragile states are often characterised by ongoing violence and insecurity, a legacy of conflict, weak governance and the inability to deliver the efficient and equitable distribution of public goods. They have consistently grown more slowly than other low-income countries, and the rate of extreme poverty is rising within them. They lag behind in human development indicators; with a 50% higher prevalence of malnutrition, 20% higher child mortality, and 18% lower primary education completion rates than other low-income countries. In its report, 'World Development Report 2011: Overview', the World Bank states that some 1.5 billion people live in countries affected by repeated cycles of political and criminal violence. This report argues that breaking these cycles involves a) strengthening legitimate national institutions and governance to meet citizens' key needs; and b) alleviating international stresses that increase the risks of conflict (such as food price volatility and infiltration by trafficking networks).

A study was made by the Institute of Development Studies on 'How Does State Fragility Affect Rural Development?'. The study operationalizes the concept of state fragility as, "States are fragile when they suffer major authority and/or legitimacy and capacity deficits, diminishing their ability to provide the basic functions needed for poverty reduction and development and to safeguard the security and human rights of their populations [in urban and rural areas]". Using Afghanistan, the Democratic Republic of the Congo (DRC), Yemen, Nepal and Bolivia as country cases, the evidence presented in this study suggests that there are some particular and big challenges for rural development in fragile states. State fragility –disaggregated along the dimensions of state authority, legitimacy and capacity –affects levels of rural poverty, public service delivery and violence against women in a number of ways, making the achievement of rural development on the whole more difficult. The lack or limitations of development in rural areas in fragile countries, in turn, enhances the fragility of the state overall, creating a kind of vicious circle of fragility that is difficult to break.

The following key findings of the above study strengthen our assertion that if state legitimacy suffers, then human development also suffers.

Key findings:

- Extensive rural poverty is both related to (a) significant deficits in state authority, legitimacy and capacity, particularly in settings with violent conflict (and associated external interventions); and (b) persisting high levels of social inequality and ethnic cleavages in states where authority and capacity deficits are less pronounced.

- Social inequalities between rural and urban areas are related to authority and capacity deficits, including the absence of strong, consistent and legitimate political leadership, and a historical urban elite bias.

- The provision of social welfare safety nets by non-state, traditional and customary organizations, including with respect to basic food security in rural areas, is related to state authority and capacity deficits, and deepens existing legitimacy deficits.

- Particularly in fragile settings affected by violent conflict, deficits in state authority result in increased pauperization of rural populations due to the disruption of rural livelihoods and wage-labour migration.

- Uncertain status of land tenure and land ownership in rural areas is related to, and compounded by, deficits in state authority and capacity.

- Ineffective service delivery in rural areas is found in countries with both higher and lower deficits in state authority and capacity, and it undermines state legitimacy.

- Higher levels of violence against women in rural areas are possibly related to deficits in state authority and capacity, particularly because of the absence or weakness of formal justice institutions and the prevalence of traditional and customary authorities.

- Food insecurity in rural regions is significantly affected by state fragility. [4]

Nancy Lindborg, President, United States Institute of Peace confirms the strong connection between lack of legitimacy and fragile condition of a state explaining that fragility is the absence or breakdown of the social contract between people and their government. Fragile states suffer deficits of institutional capacity and political legitimacy that increase the risk of instability and violent conflict, sapping the state of resilience to disruptive shocks. The source of this state-society dysfunction—fragility—can be an absence of legitimacy, effectiveness, or both. Legitimacy is weakened when institutions are not inclusive or responsive to all identity groups, including minority and marginalized populations. Repressive, corrupt states undermine citizens' confidence in government. Effectiveness is diminished when state-society interactions fail to meet their citizens' needs and expectations for security, health, economic wellbeing, and social welfare. High levels of fragility—whether caused by ineffectiveness, illegitimacy, or both—create enabling conditions for armed conflict and political instability. [5]

Armed with information and communication technology, people of countries governed with lack of sufficient legitimacy started questioning their rulers by different movements. One such movement is the Arab Spring commenced in 2010. As the result of these movements, the rule of Col. Muammar Gaddafi came to an end in Libya and Hosni Mubarak lost his power in Egypt in 2011. But the huge sufferings of the citizens of such countries before and after the change in government due to lack of state legitimacy go unnoticed and remain irreversible. Nobody can tell what sort of legitimacy is enjoyed now by the present rulers of North Korea, Afghanistan, Syria, Yemen, South Sudan, Somalia, Myanmar and many other fragile nations. Wherever there is deficiency in the legitimacy of the rulers, the state's stability, social order, peace and development become questionable and the citizens suffer from lack of political and economic freedom, liberty and overall growth. This is why the state legitimacy assumes great importance in all spheres of life, even though it is ignored for international accreditation as a state. It is unfortunate that state once formed always maintains its political identity, whatever be the credibility, constitution and nature of the ruling government and howsoever the citizens of the state suffer!

STATE LEGITIMACY – ASSESSMENT

Though some kind of political legitimacy is claimed by the rulers of all states, there is no established framework to judge whether such legitimacy is valid, functional and to the expected level of non-coercive approval of the citizens. Absence of a rational mechanism to assess the validity and efficacy of state legitimacy internally and externally is perceived as the major cause for the existence of many fragile and conflict affected countries and deplorable condition of millions of people living in them. In democracies where fair elections are held and the government is formed with majority, no separate mechanism is required to assess the legitimacy of the government. But the number of such democratic countries are in minority and this number is also diminishing nowadays, by holding rigged and manipulated elections.

The concept of state legitimacy has gone under the scrutiny of many political scientists and they have formulated certain useful theoretical approaches. Accordingly, there are three general types and dimensions of legitimacy that pertain to the state: i) how the state functions (input legitimacy): the legitimacy of the state is here tied to the rules and procedures through which it makes binding decisions (participatory processes, bureaucratic management, justice); ii) what the state does (output): legitimacy is defined in relation to the perceived effectiveness and quality of the services it delivers; iii) What kinds of beliefs allow people to take the state as the rightful authority and to share a sense of community and identity intimately related to the state. [6]

Further, there are two more principal approaches to assess the legitimacy. One is concerned with normative standards to which an actor, institution or political order must conform in order to be considered legitimate. In this approach there is a right way that an actor, institution or political order should exercise power. The second approach treats legitimacy or the 'rightness of an authority' as being determined by both the governed and the authorities in a given society. This approach tends to focus on the perceptions which people hold about an actor, institution or political order, but is also concerned with the factors that incentivise a society to consent to power.

It is useful to identify which approach is being used, because an entity could be described as both legitimate and illegitimate based on whether a normative or empirical approach is being used. A state could be considered legitimate by its citizens, for example, despite failing to conform to the normative definition based on features such as democratic elections and respect for human rights, or vice-versa. In everyday use of the term legitimacy in the media and in development, the state institutional-normative approach is often used to evaluate the legitimacy of states. The state institutional-normative approach is less relevant for evaluating armed non-state actors, although normative evaluations of non-state actors are often made based on the same values. Thus, the Free Syrian Army is judged to be legitimate by international actors because it advocates a secular democratic state and the protection of human rights, whereas ISIL is judged to be illegitimate as it advocates an Islamic state and does not adhere to the liberal concept of human rights.

In his exploration of how to think about legitimacy and illegitimacy, Robert Lamb (2014) emphasises the importance of not only identifying what entity is being evaluated for legitimacy/illegitimacy (which he termed the 'conferee') but who is making that judgement (the 'referee'). It follows that the legitimacy of individual actors, political parties, states or political settlements will vary according to who the referee is. Using the normative approach to evaluating legitimacy, the referee is the evaluator himself/herself whereas, in the empirical approach, the referee is the population over which the conferee exerts authority. [7]

From the above discussions, it is clear that empirical approach is preferable to normative one to assess the state legitimacy. Various models are being considered to quantify the measure of state legitimacy periodically by political analysts. But so far, no internationally approved methodology has been evolved. Further, there is no agreed set of actions to be followed on the basis of such assessment. Though everyone is aware of the different humanitarian, political, economic and social problems the fragile states are facing, no international efforts are taken to address the crucial contributing factor of their lack of state legitimacy, except arranging human development aids to underprivileged communities of these states. But with dysfunctional government, it is difficult to undertake human aid activities. Like in the case of climate change, no international action has been planned to strengthen the legitimacy of such states by prescribing minimum qualifying standards for state legitimacy.

STATE LEGITIMACY – QUANTIFICATION

In absence of an internationally approved methodology to quantify the state legitimacy, let us discuss some well recognized global assessments of various factors closely associated with the legitimacy and ranking of states based on such assessment, done by reputed organizations by using both 'input' and 'output' methodologies. To a greater extent, these indices reflect the degree of political legitimacy of a state.

Fragile State Index (FSI)

The Fund for Peace, an American non-profit, non-governmental research and educational institution is the only organization which quantifies the legitimacy parameters of states and publishes Fragile State Index every year. According to its methodology, the State Legitimacy Indicator considers the representativeness and openness of government and its relationship with its citizenry. The Indicator looks at the population's level of confidence in state institutions and processes, and assesses the effects where that confidence is absent, manifested through mass public demonstrations, sustained civil disobedience, or the rise of armed insurgencies. Though the State Legitimacy indicator does not necessarily make a judgment on democratic governance, it does consider the integrity of elections where they take place (such as flawed or boycotted elections), the nature of political transitions, and where there is an absence of democratic elections, the degree to which the government is representative of the population of which it governs. The Indicator takes into account openness of government, specifically the openness of ruling elites to transparency, accountability and political representation, or conversely the levels of corruption, profiteering, and marginalizing, persecuting, or otherwise excluding opposition groups. The Indicator also considers the ability of a state to exercise basic functions that infer a population's confidence in its government and institutions, such as through the ability to collect taxes.

The Funds for Peace's Annual Report 2020 has categorised the states in the following manner, in its Fragile State Index: [8]

Group	Number of countries
Very sustainable	11
Sustainable	7
Very stable	13
More stable	31

Group	Number of countries
Warning	31
Elevated warning	30
High warning	24
Alert	22
High alert	5
Very high alert	4

The legitimacy of 55 countries which are grouped at the bottom four classifications will have to be assumed as weak and the governments in these states are lacking people's consent.

Human Development Index (HDI)

Human Development Index (HDI) is yet another important yearly ranking of performance of countries done by the United Nations Development Programme (UNDP), which can throw light on some important aspects of output efficiency of states. The Human Development Index (HDI) is a statistic composite index of life expectancy, education (Literacy Rate, Gross Enrolment Ratio at different levels and Net Attendance Ratio), and per capita income indicators, which are used to rank countries into four tiers of human development. According to HDI 2020, the number of countries classified under these four levels are as under: [9]

Tier	Number of countries
Very High Human Development	66
High Human Development	53
Medium Human Development	37
Low Human Development	33

Based on this critical ranking of human development progress, one can assume that the state legitimacy of about 33 countries grouped under 'Low Human Development' is frail and contentious and these states are run by dysfunctional governments.

Fragile and Conflict-affected Situations (FCS)

The list of Fragile and Conflict-affected Situations (FCS) is released annually by the World Bank Group (WBG). The list distinguishes between countries based on the nature and severity of issues they face. The classification uses the following categories:

Countries with high levels of institutional and social fragility, identified based on publicly available indicators that measure the quality of policy and institutions and manifestations of fragility.

Countries affected by violent conflict, identified based on a threshold number of conflict-related deaths relative to the population. This category includes two sub-categories based on the intensity of violence: countries in high-intensity conflict and countries in medium-intensity conflict.

The FY21 List of Fragile and Conflict-affected Situations reveals the following groups: [10]

Classification	Number of states
High intensity conflict	4
Medium intensity conflict	13
High institutional and social fragility	
Non-small states	15
Small states	7

Governments in all the above 39 countries cannot have proper control over its mandatory functions and therefore, the state legitimacy of such nations is very much doubtful.

Economics Freedom Index

Another important quantification relating to state legitimacy is done by the Heritage Foundation in the course of preparation of its Economics Freedom Index. According to the Foundation, economic freedom is the fundamental right of every human to control his or her own labour and property. In an economically free society, individuals are free to work, produce, consume, and invest in any way they please. In economically free societies, governments allow labour, capital, and goods to move freely, and refrain from coercion or constraint of liberty beyond the extent necessary to protect and maintain liberty itself. It measures economic freedom based on 12 quantitative and qualitative factors, grouped into four broad categories, or pillars, of economic freedom:

- Rule of Law (property rights, government integrity, judicial effectiveness)

- Government Size (government spending, tax burden, fiscal health)

- Regulatory Efficiency (business freedom, labour freedom, monetary freedom)

- Open Markets (trade freedom, investment freedom, financial freedom)

The above factors would greatly reflect upon the legitimacy of a state.

2020 Index of Economic Freedom has assembled the countries as follows: [11]

Group	Number of countries
Free	6
Mostly Free	31
Moderately Free	62
Mostly Unfree	62
Repressed	19
Not Ranked	6

In the above grouping, governments of 62 mostly unfree, 19 repressed and 6 not ranked countries cannot said to be enjoying a reasonable degree of state legitimacy.

Corruption Perception Index (CPI)

The CPI scores and ranks countries/territories based on how corrupt a country's public sector is perceived to be by experts and business executives. It is a composite index determined with a combination of 13 surveys and assessments of corruption, collected by a variety of reputable institutions. The CPI is the most widely used indicator of corruption worldwide. According to the 2020 CPI, of the 180 countries ranked, about two-thirds of countries score below 50/100 on this year's CPI, with an average score of just 43/100. About 32 countries scored 25/100 and less. [12]

It is no surprise that most of the bottom listed countries in all the above indices are almost the same. List of 50 countries at the bottom in the Fragile State Index (FSI) 2020 with their corresponding assessment made in other indices discussed above is given in **Annexure – I**. FY20 List of Fragile and Conflict-affected Situations is furnished in **Annexure – II**. If the present political and socio-economic conditions of the countries listed in the above annexures are examined, it would give a fair idea as to how the lack of political legitimacy of the governments of these countries has led to the current deprived conditions of their citizens.

Prof. Bruce Gilley introduced a novel multidimensional, quantitative measure of the qualitative concept of political legitimacy in his 2006 article "The meaning and measure of state legitimacy: results for 72 countries", which is extended by other scholars. In the quantification methodology suggested by Gilley as well as the methodologies of the global indices discussed above, assessment of political, administrative, social and economic factors of the state only have been considered, based on the classical definition for state legitimacy. But today in the globalized world, the impact of state legitimacy extends beyond the national borders of a state.

ENLARGING DOMAIN OF STATE LEGITIMACY

Lack of state legitimacy and consequential dysfunctional government not only affect the interest of its citizens, but with its fragile nature, such state leaves negative impact on other states too. Fragile states have been linked with a range of transnational security threats and humanitarian concerns including mass migration, organised crime, violent conflict, communicable diseases, environmental degradation and, more recently, terrorism. Some argue fragile states have direct 'spill-over' effects on neighbouring countries, including reduced growth and destabilisation. The negative impacts of fragility across borders are often considered as justification for international intervention. [13]

Forced migration from fragile nations to neighbouring and far off countries has recently emerged as a major international human crisis. Following are considered as the main causes of forced migration, which are mainly prevalent in all fragile and conflict affected countries:

Conflict-Induced Displacement occurs when people are forced to flee their homes as a result of armed conflict including civil war, generalized violence, and persecution on the grounds of nationality, race, religion, political opinion or social group.

Development-Induced Displacement occurs when people are compelled to move as a result of policies and projects implemented to advance 'development' efforts. Examples of this include large-scale infrastructure projects such as dams, roads, ports, airports; urban clearance initiatives; mining and deforestation; and the introduction of conservation parks/reserves and biosphere projects.

Disaster-Induced Displacement occurs when people are displaced as a result of natural disasters (floods, volcanoes, landslides, earthquakes), environmental change (deforestation, desertification, land degradation, global warming) and human-made disasters (industrial accidents, radioactivity).

According to the UNHCR, there were 79.5 million people forcibly displaced worldwide in 2019. Of them, 45.7 million people displaced within the state. The rest were refugees and asylum seekers in foreign countries. If the host country of migrants happens to be another fragile nation, its social and economic stress gets added. It is said that immigration to developed nations has both positive and negative impacts. On the negative side, people of host countries consider that the immigration of people from other countries is dangerous for their personal security, as well as a threat for the economy and the culture of their country. They think that the massive influx of immigrants in their country will increase the threat of terrorism and the crime rates. They also believe that handling immigration poses a huge financial burden for receiving countries. Fragile countries with religious activities are considered as breeding ground for terrorists as they nurture many violent religious fundamentalist groups. 9/11 attacks confirmed this fact.

International agencies, State governments and business organizations dealing with a fragile state find it difficult to make such state to comply with the mutually agreed contractual obligations. With the ongoing armed conflicts, displacing population, weak infrastructure and poor state administrative machinery, the international aid agencies struggle to execute the human development projects in fragile and conflict affected countries.

Conflicts are increasingly turning international and therefore much harder to solve, providing proxy ground for external powers to manipulate fragile institutions, exercise their own interests, and flex their muscles. These conflicts are lasting longer and costing more: various estimates of the costs of global conflict range from $9 trillion to $13.6 trillion per year. Fragile states often lack the institutional capacity to respond quickly and effectively to control the spread of pandemic disease outbreaks. With the experience of an outbreak of Ebola in Guinea, Liberia, and Sierra Leone in 2015, and the more recent outbreak of Zika in parts of Latin America, the specter of uncontrolled pandemics has never loomed larger. [14]

Rising waves of complications of fragile and conflict affected states have already crossed their borders and touched the shores of other nations. Therefore, lack of legitimacy in a state is no more a local issue of that state. It is a sneakily rising international problem. Today, it is not sufficient for a government to get the approval of its authority by majority of its citizens alone to claim political legitimacy. This process will get completed only if it gets the approval from most of the international actors with whom it interacts explicitly or impliedly in its natural and legal course of interactions.

COMPREHENSIVE AND SELF-ENFORCEABLE STATE LEGITIMACY

In view of the enlarging scope of state legitimacy, to have a multidimensional and clear view of the political condition of a state, a comprehensive 360 degree assessment of the state legitimacy is required. This assessment work may be entrusted with a newly formed international agency monitored by the UN. This agency may work independently or along with the agencies like the World Bank Group and UNDP, which are already in the process of quantifying and ranking the countries on the basis of certain parameters relating to state legitimacy and human development. Such assessment and quantification methodology may normalise and factor in the assessment scores of the following well accepted rankings and indices closely associated with state legitimacy.

1. Fragile State Index

2. Human Development Index

3. List of Fragile and Conflict-affected Situations (FCS)

4. Economics Freedom Index

5. Corruption Perception Index

As discussed earlier, legitimacy of a state matters to international community also. To enable to make a comprehensive 360 degree assessment of state legitimacy, besides considering the above indices, an empirical assessment of its approval by other states including neighbouring states, international agencies, voluntary organizations, MNCs, financial institutions etc., which interacted with or got impacted by that state during the period of study will have to be done and appropriately incorporated in the assessment of state legitimacy. Separate surveys and methodology will have to be evolved to make such empirical assessment with reference to each entity mentioned above. An element should also be added to the methodology to evaluate and quantify the efforts taken by the state in safeguarding and upgrading its environment and following the guidelines of the Intergovernmental Panel on Climate Change (IPCC) in reducing global warming.

Mere publication of such comprehensive assessment with scores and ranking of state legitimacy will not serve any purpose, unless such index is validated by a resolution of all the members of the UN, with appropriate action plan (remedial or sanctions) to handle the countries scoring less than a threshold limit to be fixed every year. The states which help the low scored nations, violating the guidelines of such action plan should also be dealt with some kind of international sanction. Besides giving an insight into the legitimacy status of the government to its citizens, this score of a state will be useful for the policy makers of other states, international agencies and business organizations in dealing with that state. This may be a huge task to begin and there may also be opposition from international actors who want the fragile and conflict situation to continue in some states to serve their interests. But, once this process begins, it will surely self-enforce the social, political, administrative, economic and environmental discipline among all states. This comprehensive and self-enforceable mechanism to monitor state legitimacy, coupled with proper arms control measures will greatly reduce the internal and international armed conflicts too. In this globalized world, majority of the states and international institutions and organizations and MNCs would welcome this initiative, as this would simplify their decision-making process greatly in dealing with a particular state. The lapse committed in the Peace of Westphalia by not integrating the vital element of political legitimacy while conceiving sovereign state can be rectified now by this simple process of prescribing a 360° comprehensive and self-enforceable state legitimacy assessment mechanism. This effort would go a long way in ensuring consistent human development in every state and a peacefully sustainable world order.

5

NATIONALISM TO RIGHT-WING POPULISM

NATIONALISM – MISSION COMPLETE

European Origin of Nationalism

The Peace of Westphalia signed in 1648 in Germany conceived the new Westphalian state system introducing the principle of state sovereignty and thereby bringing in hitherto non existing international order in Europe. At the same time, it failed to prescribe the process of demonstrating the political legitimacy of the then monarch rulers, which would have made them accountable to their citizens to some extent. Alternatively, the rulers could have evolved some self-regulatory mechanism by themselves or provided a reasonably tolerable governance to gain the confidence of their citizens. But it did not happen. In result, the general public had to suffer a lot by the unchecked and unregulated misrule of monarchs. These developments made the emerging class of wealthy and educated elites of the society to think that it was the appropriate time for them to replace the monarchs and rule the states with the then emerging and popular political ideologies of the Enlightenment Era. The above factors culminated and resulted in action initially in France and manifested as French Revolution in late 19th century.

French Revolution was mainly influenced by the ideals of the Age of Reason or the Enlightenment that flourished in Europe in the 17th and 18th centuries. Enlightenment thinkers of Europe questioned traditional authority and embraced the notion that humanity could be improved through rational change. This philosophy was expressed in the slogan "Liberty! Equality! Fraternity!" of the French Revolution. American Revolution (against British colonialism) (1775–1783) was also a motivating factor for the French Revolution. Misgovernance of King Luis-XVI of France, segregation of middle class in the society and rising economic power of elites too contributed to the French Revolution. The French Revolution began in 1789 and the First French Republic was established in 1792 replacing the monarchy rule. This led to the execution of the king of France Louis XVI in 1793, and an extended period of political turmoil marked with violence. The above chaotic situation led to the appointment of Napoleon as First Consul of France in 1799. He was the first person who attempted to unify the continent of Europe and form a European government applying the core principles of French Revolution.

Napoleon and his armies traversed Europe from 1803 to 1815 aimed to unite the continent and bring it under French control. In this effort, he involved common French people also by fanning the sentiments of public in the name of French nationalism which made them to think that it was their onus to expand the new found political culture of France across Europe. Coercive methodologies were also used to get the support of the public for the French nationalism. Thus, Napoleon sowed the seed of nationalism corresponding to a state (France) in Europe and as he was crossing the continent, he unknowingly spread his idea of nationalism inviting negative as well as positive reaction from other states and societies of Europe.

To curtail the after effect of the French Revolution, the Congress of Vienna was held in 1814–15 and the goal was not simply to restore the old boundaries of European nations but to resize the main powers so that they could balance each other and remain at peace. The leaders were conservatives with little use for republicanism or revolution, both of which threatened to upset the status quo in Europe. The Congress of Vienna repressed nationalism and revolutions for almost a century to maintain the political status quo in Europe, which had the paradoxical effect of spreading nationalism even further. The Revolutions of 1848 used nationalism to replace the monarchy (never to return) and to establish a republican regime based on universal manhood suffrage. It changed the leadership and political landscape in countries like Austria, France, Prussia, and Spain. Germany and Italy joined this club much later. Thus, nationalism changed Europe as a whole.

Global Spread of Nationalism – Mission Complete

Political ideology of nationalism was evolved as the first pragmatic process to challenge the status-quo of monarchy allowed to be continued in the newly developed Westphalian state system with more and unrestrained power. Instead of finding ways for generating or approving much required political legitimacy in the existing states, new states called nation states were formed by gathering the people of a specified territory on some commonly shared identity and thereby creating 'popular legitimacy' to such newly formed nation states. In this process, many wars were fought to expand the territory of a nation state to consolidate the people of same national identity and to safeguard the interest of their nationalities living in other states. This process compromised the Westphalian concept of sovereignty, i.e., non-interference in other state's affairs, and such deviated sovereignty for the sake of public was termed as 'popular sovereignty'. The newly conceptualised nation state with 'popular legitimacy' and 'popular sovereignty' captured the attention of the people worldwide and new nation states came into existence across the world by wars and revolutions. This concept of nation state was also exported to other parts of the world by European colonization.

Nationalism is not an ancient political concept as portrayed by the present hyper-nationalistic political leaders. It is a modern idea conceptualised after the birth of Westphalian state system in 1648, which introduced sovereign state system. Without a sovereign state with fixed territory and population, the idea of nationalism could not have germinated. Throughout history, people have been attached to their native soil, to the traditions of their parents and communities, and to the established territorial authorities. But it was not until the end of the 18th century that nationalism began to be a generally recognized sentiment moulding public and private life and one of the great, if not the greatest, single determining factors of modern history. Because of its dynamic vitality and its all-pervading character, nationalism is often thought to be very old; sometimes it is mistakenly regarded as a permanent factor in political behaviour. Actually, the American and French revolutions of the 18th century may be regarded as its first powerful manifestations of nationalism. After penetrating the new countries of Latin America, it spread in the early 19th century to central Europe and from there, toward the middle of the century, to eastern and south-eastern Europe. At the beginning of the 20th century, nationalism flowered in Asia and Africa. Thus, the 19th century has been called the age of nationalism in Europe, while the 20th century witnessed the rise and struggle of powerful national movements throughout Asia and Africa. [1]

The European classic nationalism instilled the idea of putting the interest of the nation ahead of their own personal interest among people. It also recognized different nationalities and nation states. In this sense, nationalism was particularistic, populistic and exclusive and it celebrated differences. These attractive ideals of nationalism propelled the process of formation of nation states from 55 in 1945 to 193 in 2011. Right now, except a very few national movements, like Catalan, Kurdish and Scottish independence movements, there are not much ethnic or culture-based demands for formation of new nation state. There is also a limitation to the process of endlessly identifying new groups of nationality and to form new nation states balkanizing the existing politically stable states. Consequently, the process of formation of nation state that started at the end of the 18th century in Europe has almost come to an end at the beginning of 21st century. The mission of the classic nationalism aimed at forming new states with newly identified nationalities is complete now. All-round development of the world from the end of World War-II has shifted the political focus from nation state to people. Consequently, beyond its primary mandate, the spirit of nationalism is misapplied nowadays focusing people rather than state, in different ways, in different countries to suit the political convenience of populist political groups and vested interests of non-state actors. Therefore, violence and conflicts historically associated with the nationalism refuse to die and the symptoms of behavioural disorder of state continue to manifest across the world even today.

CURRENT PSEUDO NATIONALISM

The classic nationalism attempted to organize people sharing a common identity such as ethnicity, culture, language and historical experience primarily to form a nation state with artificially created popular political legitimacy. This unifying force helped the nation to become strong and unassailable. On the contrary, emotional appeal of nationalism is now applied at micro level within the state and society in many countries on the basis of religious, ethnic and sectarian divisions and rivalries, with intentions other than forming a new state. This kind of **pseudo nationalism** attempts to capture power in the existing state or to destabilise the state at the instance of other states or local or outside non-state actors or for financial gains of radical groups or to keep the state in chaotic conditions purposefully by the ruler to remain in power. These localised nationalistic forces are responsible for the ongoing violence in many countries of Sub-Saharan Africa, Middle East and South Asia. This kind of religious pseudo nationalism justifies the violence of ISIS, Taliban, Boko Haram, Al-Qaeda and other religious terrorist outfits perpetrated against civilians all over the world. This derailed nationalism instead making the state strong and united, promotes civil war and armed conflicts within the state, which expose the civilians to violence. There has been huge local as well as interstate displacement of people due to unliveable conditions of these states. With these prevailing conditions, 80% of the world population facing extreme poverty is expected to live in these countries in near future. The above described pseudo nationalism has reversed the core idea of nationalism, i.e., formation of a nation state by integrating people. Rather it attempts to disintegrate and disturb the society and collapse the state making the government weak and dysfunctional. Except the process of organizing people on some shared identity and fanning their sentiments, there is nothing common between classic and pseudo nationalism.

EMERGENCE OF NEO-NATIONALISM

As discussed above, the classic nationalism originated in Europe was the motivating force behind formation of many nation states across the world in the 19th and 20th centuries and pseudo nationalism is prevalent even now in many fragile and conflict affected countries weakening the state machinery. A third version of nationalism called neo-nationalism is growing today besides the pseudo nationalism.

Starting from 1989, globalization, fast growing economies, armed conflicts, international terrorism, mass immigration, climate change, etc., have diverted the attention of political leaders from their creative ideas on formation of new nation states. When the ordinary people started losing their interest in the classical elements of nation formation and getting increasingly involved in the emerging national and global issues, the politicians began to search for new fuel to ignite the passion of nationalism among them, highlighting old but neglected and resurfacing issues, in reaction to the above global developments, for their electoral gains. This is how the world is facing the wave of **neo-nationalism** or **national populism** today. As the impact of globalization, free market, immigration, terrorism and climate change varies from country to country, the reactionary agenda of neo-nationalists also differs. In the US, which pioneered the policies of pluralism, international liberalism and multiculturalism, Donald Trump could emerge as the president despite his controversial statements about

Mexican immigrants, Muslims, refugees, women, and other minorities. He was a polarizing figure within the uncharted territory of Islamophobia, xenophobia, racism, and misogyny and still could give a tough contest in the recent election to the Democratic party candidate Joe Biden. British Prime Minister Boris Johnson gave a hard blow to the globalization by leaving the European Union with BREXIT. In country like India, though the impact from the above factors is not significant and in spite of the fact that globalization actually accelerated its economy, national populism has picked up its pace in the form of Hindu nationalism in recent years. Jair Bolsonaro, a far-right politician known for making homophobic and misogynist statements and supporting neoliberal policies and military dictatorship, won Brazil's presidential election. Identity crisis of man in the age of increasing income, wealth and abundance as the result of economic liberalism is also said to be the cause for attraction to identity seeking populistic ideas. Some argue that declining faith of people in government make them lean towards populistic narratives. Generally, all neo-nationalistic movements are populists attracting common people and are against elites and liberal international order.

TYPES OF NATIONALISM

As the term nationalism is used and understood today in different ways in different perspectives and in different contexts, it is better to redefine the term with reference to its diverse applications based on the above discussion to enable to distinguish their characteristic and functional identities for our further discussions.

Uniting people on some shared common identity for formation of a new nation state and keeping the individual's interest subject to the national interest may be called **'Classic Nationalism'**.

Grouping people on some shared common identity, without the intension of forming a new nation state, but for disrupting the existing structure and functions of a state to serve some vested interests may be termed as **'Pseudo Nationalism'**.

If people are organized on some shared common ideas to polarize the society of a state, prioritising the interest of an identified group (populism) over the common interest of the state and the world community may be labelled as '**Neo-Nationalism**'. It is also termed as 'national populism'.

SHADES OF POPULISM

According to Ezaz Ahmed, the phenomenon of populism has been one of the most discounted political jargons of the 21st century. It has been the most talked about yet misunderstood trend in recent times. There has been a steady surge of populist leaders from divergent ideologies coming to power in countries as diverse as India, Hungary, Brazil, Philippines and Italy. Swathes of populist leaders have taken the entire spectrum of socio-political affairs by storm. Although there is no universally agreed upon definition by political scientists, populism loosely means a political approach that seemingly strives to emancipate ordinary people who feel their concerns are disregarded by the ruling elite. Populism comes in many forms that are as different as apples and oranges. Hence, it is futile to compare one populist leader with another, let alone put them all in one compartment.

The right one

A common denominator of populism is to create notions of exclusivity amongst the electorate. And what defines the right-leaning populist leaders is that they aim to restrict and strengthen their support by focusing specially on social citizenship rights of a certain group of nationals against 'others' such as immigrants, foreign entities and apparently intrusive inter-governmental organisations. Domestic as well as external enemies are also considered to be threats to national security and integrity in economic and socio-political terms. To overcome such threats and put the nation & its 'people' first is fundamental to the populist agenda.

What the likes of Donald Trump and Nigel Farage express through their "Make America Great Again" and "Leave" campaigns is to restrict the national identity of 'the people' which clearly excludes refugees, immigrants and others defined as 'foreign' to the predefined ideal that they propound. Populists on this side of the aisle tend to claim that their version of the 'people' needs more representation. They champion the people against the elites that they accuse of favouring a third group that comprises of immigrants, Islamists or African Americans. The operative substances in their rhetoric are established elites, the other people and 'nation first' at all costs. They also invoke a sense of morality in their cause, thereby evoking conscience on a much deeper level. It arouses people's sentiments on moral grounds that paints the leader as a saviour and he/she is worshipped in a god-like fashion. This moralisation of ideology or the leader translates into voter consolidation wherein citizens vote en-masse with little to no rationale to back their respective political choice.

Right-wing populism itself comes in a variety of forms. For instance, in the United States, populists have gained traction largely, though not exclusively, through anti-immigration policies. In India, religious/ethnic and nationalist/ethnic versions of 'the people' have resonated and focused more strongly on the corruption of elites. Although, this difference is a matter varying only in degree, broadly speaking, a nationalist and anti-elite agenda, as well as the demand for more 'true' representation is characteristic of populism of all kinds.

The left way out

Populist leaders on the left focus on economically superior elites — who, according to them, continue to suppress the majority of the population to perpetually keep themselves in the echelons of power. For the leftist populist, one of the main factors that keep making the rich even richer is globalisation and that is where they tend to exploit sentiments and call for nationalist policies that include more economic barriers. To quote historian Michael Kazin, populist leaders subscribing to the left ideology "use a language that conceives of ordinary people as a noble assemblage not bounded narrowly by class; view their elite opponents as self-serving and undemocratic, and seek to mobilise the former against the latter."

Left wing populists champion the people against an elite or an establishment. Theirs is a vertical politics of the bottom and middle, arrayed against the top. They are in constant conflict with the establishment and the demands that come out of it are, to say the least, utopian. Exclusionary politics is not identical to just the right; left-wing populist leaders exclude not people but sectors of the establishment that are in the service of neo-liberal global corporations.

Populists at home, globalists abroad

As a consequence of the increasingly intermingling policies between the left and right; and shrinking of spaces to channelise people's grievances in liberal democracies around the world, populism has become an effective way to take the people's demands into account. However, it is important to note that populist leaders, even when exclusivists domestically, tend to be globalists on the international front. Bilateral and multilateral events are where they demonstrate their eagerness to bring in more foreign trade and investment into their respective countries because they know that it would positively stimulate the economy and benefit the people. [2] At present, the right-wing populism is on the rise globally.

RISING RIGHT-WING POPULISM

Quartz's reporter Annalisa Merelli reports that right-wing populism, the leitmotiv of contemporary politics, is on the rise. It certainly feels that way: Starting in the mid-2010s, democracies all over the world have turned toward the right, electing representatives that stand in stark contrast to those that pushed for globalization and international cooperation two decades earlier. Right-wing populism isn't a monolith. It has different features in different countries. It's hard, and somewhat simplistic, to ascribe all of the parties, movements, and leaders emerging in this historic shift to a single political trend. Yet, they do have some elements in common. The movements and parties that belong to it share xenophobic, nationalistic traits, a tendency toward authoritarianism, aggressive leadership, and an anti-elitist message. All over Europe, the past few years have seen a noticeable growth in xenophobia, particularly in reaction to asylum seekers and immigrants. Simultaneously, there's been a growing rejection of European cooperation, propelling the 2016 vote in favor of Brexit in the UK, and the rise of far-right movements all over the continent. In the United States, president Donald Trump—whose rise to power was helped by right-wing populist strategist Steve Bannon—has promoted an anti-immigrant agenda. The American president has not shied away from incendiary comments and under his presidency hate crimes are on the rise. In India, meanwhile, voters elected prime minister Narendra Modi, a Hindu nationalist, in 2014 and then again earlier this year. His latest government is enforcing an agenda that threatens minorities and rallies the Hindu majority around the goal of abandoning secularism. How quickly right-wing populism has spread globally, or at least in the countries with democratic systems, is remarkable. When this decade began, hardly any of the parties and leaders that now run the world, or appear set to, were on anyone's radar. Now these movements are spreading quickly. Among the world's democracies, a growing number has embraced right-wing populism, and either have governments led by populist parties, or supported by them.

According to her, in 20 nations right-wing populist parties are in government. (**Annexure-III**) In several other countries, too, right-wing populist parties are gaining traction, and are set to become main players, or form governments, in the near future. She has listed 13 such countries, which surprisingly includes the world's most robust democracies Denmark, Finland and Sweden. [3]

Dr Matthew Lockwood of University of Sussex contends that one potential explanation rests on an analysis of populism as a response to structural change in the global economy. In this approach, emphasis is given to the fact that right-wing populist parties have had particular appeal amongst those – especially male, industrial and manufacturing workers and those in less skilled white-collar occupations – whose jobs, incomes and wider economic security have been most eroded by processes of globalisation, automation and de-unionisation. Political scientist Hans-Georg Betz has called this group the 'losers of modernisation', and more recently they have been referred to in the media as the 'left behind'. This group have not only been unable to benefit from the rise of the knowledge economy, but they have also lost their political voice, as mainstream political parties have become more technocratic and converged on a policy agenda aimed at middle-class voters, creating a 'cartelisation' of politics. On this view, the 'left behind' have disproportionately rallied around populist parties precisely because they stand outside the consensus. [4]

Weakening Democracy

The rise of nationalism and populism in recent years has caused a rift in economics, environmental factors, issues regarding income, and governments globally. Nationalism is the belief that nations would benefit from acting independently rather than collectively, emphasizing national rather than international goals. Indeed, nationalism has historically amalgamated governments and sparked revolutions because of its unifying tendencies. In addition to this, populism is a philosophy directed to the needs of the common people and advocating a more equitable distribution of wealth and power. These two ideologies have proven to be both beneficial and detrimental to countries and the overall well-being of citizens; however, history ultimately indicates more detrimental trends. Furthermore, an increase in both nationalism and populism has emerged globally during about the last 75 years, but specifically in Europe. Research indicates that the recent rise in populism and nationalism has had a negative effect on the extent to which citizens trust in their governments and contributed to the weakening of representative democracy. [5]

Impact on Liberal International Order

Prof G. John Ikenberry states that for seven decades the world has been dominated by a western liberal order. After the Second World War, the United States and its partners built a multifaceted and sprawling international order, organized around economic openness, multilateral institutions, security cooperation and democratic solidarity. Along the way, the United States became the 'first citizen' of this order, providing hegemonic leadership—anchoring the alliances, stabilizing the world economy, fostering cooperation and championing 'free world' values. Western Europe and Japan emerged as key partners, tying their security and economic fortunes to this extended liberal order. After the end of the Cold War, this order spread outwards. Countries in east Asia, eastern Europe and Latin America made democratic transitions and became integrated into the world economy. As the post-war order expanded, so too did its governance institutions. NATO expanded, the WTO was launched and the G20 took centre stage. Looking at the world at the end of the twentieth century, one could be excused for thinking that history was moving in a progressive and liberal internationalist direction. Today, this liberal international order is in crisis. For the first time since the 1930s, the United States has elected a president who is actively hostile to liberal internationalism. Trade, alliances, international law, multilateralism, environment, torture and human rights—on all these issues, President Trump has made statements that, if acted upon, would effectively bring to an end America's role as leader of the liberal world order. Simultaneously, Britain's decision to leave the EU, and a myriad other troubles besetting Europe, appear to mark an end to the long post-war project of building a greater union. The uncertainties of Europe, as the quiet bulwark of the wider liberal international order, have global significance. Meanwhile, liberal democracy itself appears to be in retreat, as varieties of 'new authoritarianism' rise to new salience in countries such as Hungary, Poland, the Philippines and Turkey. Across the liberal democratic world, populist, nationalist and xenophobic strands of backlash politics have proliferated. [6]

General Negative Effects

Populists are disruptive. They position themselves as outsiders who are radically different and separate from the existing order. So, they frequently advocate for a change to the status quo and may champion the need for urgent structural change, whether that is economic or cultural. They often do this by promoting a sense of crisis (whether true or not), and presenting themselves as having the solution to the crisis. Actually, they have none.

Dr Lisa Wade lucidly explains the negative effects of nationalism and national populism as follows:

Nationalism — a passionate investment in one's country over and above others — is neither good nor neutral. Here are some reasons why it's dangerous:

- Nationalism is a form of in-group/out-group thinking. It encourages the kind of "us" vs. "them" attitude that drives sports fandom, making people irrationally committed to one team. When the team wins, they feel victorious (even though they just watched), and they feel pleasure in others' defeat.

- Committed to winning at all costs, with power-seeking and superiority as the only real goal, nationalists feel justified in hurting the people of other countries. Selfishness and a will to power — instead of morality, mutual benefit, or long-term stability — becomes the driving force of foreign policy. Broken agreements, violence, indifference to suffering, and other harms to countries and their peoples destabilize global politics.

- Nationalism also contributes to internal fragmentation and instability. It requires that we decide who is and isn't truly part of the nation, encouraging exclusionary, prejudiced attitudes and policies towards anyone within our borders who is identified as part of "them."

- A leader with a nationalist mandate will feel entitled to breaking the laws of his or her own country. If the Constitution interferes with nationalist ambition, then the Constitution can be set aside.

- A nationalist leader will have to lie and distort history in order to maintain the illusion of superiority. A nationalist regime requires a post-truth politics, one that makes facts irrelevant in favour of emotional appeals.

- Thoughtful and responsive governance interferes with self-glorification, so all internal reflection and external criticism must be squashed. Nationalist leaders attack and disempower anyone who questions the nationalist program and aim to destroy social movements. [7]

Classical nationalism artificially integrated the society in the name of shared culture, ethnicity, language, history etc., and with that unity, formed nation states. Neo-nationalism largely represented by right wing nationalism/populism attempts to divide the society of a nation state on the pretext of some socio-cultural agenda like racism, communalism, nativism, Islamophobia, Sinophobia, Euroscepticism, anti-globalization, anti-immigration, climate denialism etc. After formation of nation state, classical nationalism generally treated people of that state as 'us' and citizens of other states were treated as 'others'. Since the right-wing populism's intention is to exploit the sentiments of the common people to win elections and capture power in a state, the 'us' group and 'others' group are created within the state itself on some reactionary elements. The object of classical nationalism is diametrically opposite to that of neo-nationalism, as it aims to disturb the national cohesion bonded by the classical nationalism. Sometimes, in its extreme form, the right-wing populism touches the radical right with the characteristics of authoritarianism and fascism.

According to Prof Federico Finchelstein like fascism, populism does not recognize a legitimate political place for an opposition that it regards as acting against the desires of the people and that it also accuses of being tyrannical, conspiratorial, and antidemocratic. ... The opponents are turned into public enemies, but only rhetorically. If populism moves from rhetorical enmity to practices of enemy identification and persecution, we could be talking about its transformation into fascism or another form of dictatorial repression. This has happened in the past ... and without question it could happen in the future. This morphing of populism back into fascism is always a possibility, but it is very uncommon, and when it does happen, and populism becomes fully antidemocratic, it is no longer populism. [8]

Oxfam reports that there is increasing solidarity on the populist right and international cooperation between right-wing populist parties and politicians. This growing pattern of political collaboration and alliances includes leaders of authoritarian regimes outside of the west, and may presage major geopolitical realignments. The increasing political power of right-wing populist parties and movements threatens other core elements of rights-based agendas. For instance: tackling anthropogenic climate change and its consequences; the continuing fight for gender equality, and the expansion of LGBT rights; and the importance of scientific and secular reasoning as the basis for informing and setting public policy decision-making. Particularly troubling is that the negative values espoused by the radical right are so widely held. The politics and discourses of right-wing populism threaten civil society's space and the freedom of international organizations to speak out on behalf of vulnerable people.

Performance of Populist Governments

All populist leaders claim that they put their 'nation first'. But actually, their performance and efficacy in translating their words into deeds is dismal. The Fund For Peace Fragile State Index 2020 report narrates that initially the 2008 financial crisis unleashed a wave of populism across the world's democracies. While many political leaders and technocrats devised policies and plans to address the structural causes and help the affected, others sought villains to punish and scapegoats to banish. Later, in 2014, as millions fled war-torn Syria at an unprecedented scale, xenophobia and anti-immigration sentiment further complicated the urgency of the challenge. These two shocks have made it much more difficult to harness the political and social capital necessary to make the individual and collective sacrifices necessary to not only bounce back from shocks, but also to make fundamental changes to adjust to upheaval. According to this report, the UK, Brazil and India find 7th, 9th and 11th place in the list of 14 Most Worsened Countries 2020. Among the 20 Long-term Worsened Countries between 2010 and 2020, the UK, the USA and Brazil find place in 11th, 12th and 13th positions with the company of Libya, Syria, Yemen and Venezuela. Till March 2021, the countries most affected by COVID-19 were the USA, Brazil, India, and the UK. The one common thing among all these countries is that they are ruled by conservative and hyper-national populist regimes. The above corroborative facts indicate that performance of populist governments in all fronts of governance is inefficient and directionless in short and long-terms. In fact, they do not have any viable alternatives to the ideologies they oppose. Their policies attached to sentiments and emotions are employed only to win the elections and beyond that they become useless rhetoric to their own people and others. In short, by opposing elites and establishment they come to power. Once they become elites and part of establishment, they do not have solutions for the issues they raised.

Though the policies of populists are generally anti-progressive and against basic democratic principles such as human rights, equality, liberty, liberalism etc., their current opposition to climate positive action and immigration/refugees is a growing threat to human civilization. It is ironical, though not justifiable that the European nations which colonized most of the countries of the world and ruled for centuries against their own Westphalian principle of sovereignty are now agitating on the issues of immigration and refuges, notwithstanding the fact the such influx of foreign nationals, in fact, has economically benefitted the hosting countries too. Similarly, industrially developed countries are the biggest polluters of the world, causing catastrophic consequences of climate change. Unfortunately, the right-wing populists of these countries only are in denial mode of climate change effects and reluctant to participate in the international efforts to reduce global warming. These negative views of right-wing populism rising particularly in developed nations are likely to have immediate impact on the human development efforts in less developed countries. In long term, these anti global attitudes are going to turn against their own interest. Their withdrawal from global participation would be taken advantage by the developing nations like China and India politically and economically pushing down their economies and their present status, image and command in the world order.

6
INSIGHTISM

NEED FOR FRESH POLITICAL APPROACH

We started our discussion on the struggling human development and its connection with the major global risks i.e., climate change, extreme poverty, ever increasing economic inequality and large scale and religious conflicts, which are challenging the very survival of human civilization now and in future. With the fast-growing global wealth, achievements made in all fields of science and technology and enough manpower with expertise and skills, addressing the above challenges is theoretically possible within a reasonable timeframe. But practically, it does not happen. We noticed that the congenital and behavioural disorders of state disable the course of such achievement.

In political philosophies evolved since antiquity, state plays the pivotal role in determining the legal, political, social and economic status of its citizens. Till recently, it was said that the progress of western political philosophy had served its purpose and reached its peak and come to its historical end. Differing from this view, we have pointed out that many critical problems of the world failed to be addressed by such political theories because of their lack of inclusive and global approach and capacity to diagnose and cure the congenital and behavioural disorders of states.

American Political Philosopher Richard J. Arneson stresses the above point stating that the history of Western political philosophy from Plato to the present day makes plain that the discipline is still faced with the basic problems defined by the Greeks. The need to redeploy public power in order to maintain the survival and enhance the quality of human life, for example, has never been so essential. And, if the opportunities for promoting well-being are now far greater, the penalties for the abuse of power are nothing less than the destruction or gross degradation of all life on the planet. [1]

Western Political Philosophies are Truly Western

Though political philosophy was emerged in ancient Babylon (Hammurabi), China (Confucius) and India (Kautilya), only the western political theories germinated from Ancient Greece (Plato and Aristotle) and evolved in Europe over many centuries have continued to advance and be acknowledged globally. Europe was the birth place of the Renaissance and the Enlightenment movements and the Industrial Revolution. The French and the Russian Revolutions demonstrated the practical application of European political ideologies. The first democratic country of the world constituted in 1776, the USA adopted many then existing western political concepts from democracy to separation of powers to constitutionalism. European nations colonized the countries across the world and introduced the new political concepts of Westphalian sovereign state system and nation state across the world. Since the modern nation state system is a western political concept, naturally there was no difficulty in understanding and adapting to the western political philosophies in the rest of the world. No other political theory was evolved anywhere in the world in parallel with the western political philosophy, gaining international attention. Therefore, political philosophy today is nothing but the western political philosophy.

Political philosophy cannot be defined precisely. Generally, it is the study of topics such as politics, liberty, justice, property, rights, law, and the enforcement of laws by authority: what they are, if they are needed, what makes a government legitimate, what rights and freedoms it should protect, what form it should take, what the law is, and what duties citizens owe to a legitimate government, if any, and when it may be legitimately overthrown, if ever. [2]

Political philosophers seek to establish basic principles that will, for instance, justify a particular form of state, show that individuals have certain inalienable rights, or tell us how a society's material resources should be shared among its members. This usually involves analysing and interpreting ideas like freedom, justice, authority and democracy and then applying them in a critical way to the social and political institutions that currently exist. Some political philosophers have tried primarily to justify the prevailing arrangements of their society; others have painted pictures of an ideal state or an ideal social world that is very different from anything we have so far experienced. [3]

In spite of having such a broad scope, no western political philosophy from antiquity to contemporary deals with the political exigency of mitigating the horrible sufferings of millions of people facing abject poverty and unimaginable inequalities, notwithstanding the fact that state, the core element of political system is responsible for addressing the above woes of its citizens. Marxism addressed the plights of urban labour due to industrialisation. In the name of creating a classless and stateless society by empowering public, communism, on the contrary, strengthened the power of the state that led to authoritarian and despotic governments. Ironically, when many philosophers emphasised the duty of the state to protect the property of its citizens (from Jhon Locke to Robert Nozick), they failed to address the responsibility of the state to save the citizens from death by hunger and malnutrition. Except a very few American philosophers, all the western political philosophers were from Western Europe only and they were oblivious of or ignored the actual political and socio-economic conditions of the poor living in Africa, Asia and South America, though the people of these continents constituted majority of the population of the world. European nations which colonized many countries of these continents were well exposed to the deprived conditions of the people lived there. However, western political philosophies simply overlooked the political and economic conditions of the people in those countries and the implications of colonization. The western political thought was mainly evolved with the background and in response to the then prevailing social, political and economic conditions and aspirations of the public in Europe, more particularly Western Europe only, with European historical perspective. Even today, contemporary western political philosophies continue to be western, abstract, theoretical and normative with no practical application possible on the global problems of the day. They do not address the fast-changing and debilitating dimensions and behaviour of politics and economics of recent times, across the world.

False Presumptions

The major weakness of modern western political philosophies is that they assume legitimate democratic governments in all states of the world and that the spirit and value of democratic principles and institutions would remain intact in all democracies. That is the reason why they continue to explore the democratic principles like liberty, equality, freedom, law, justice, human rights, liberalism etc. However, the world reality is different now. Today, all states do not practice democracy and many democratic countries are not fully democratic and governments in many countries lack reasonable degree of state legitimacy. In fact, in this age of globalization and consumerism, majority of the population of the world is much bothered about their livelihood and secure and peaceful environment, rather than the form and nature of government they live under and the principles of democracy. Otherwise, there will not be roughly 30% of expatriates constituting Saudi Arabia's population, the UAE will not have 80% of its population as immigrants from 200 countries and China with 1.44 billion population, ruled by authoritarian regimes for a quite a long period cannot continue remain intact. In the present trend of global integration, people are willing to migrate to any country irrespective of its political status to earn a decent and assured livelihood.

The Democracy Index is an index compiled by the Economist Intelligence Unit (EIU), a UK-based company. It measures the state of democracy with following types of classifications:

Full democracies are nations where civil liberties and fundamental political freedoms are not only respected but also reinforced by a political culture conducive to the thriving of democratic principles.

Flawed democracies are nations where elections are fair and free and basic civil liberties are honoured but may have faults in other democratic aspects including underdeveloped political culture, low levels of participation in politics and issues in the functioning of governance.

Hybrid regimes are nations with regular electoral frauds, preventing them from being fair and free democracy. These nations commonly have governments that apply pressure on political opposition, non-independent judiciaries, widespread corruption, harassment and pressure placed on the media, anaemic rule of law.

Authoritarian regimes are nations where political pluralism has vanished or is extremely limited. These nations are often absolute monarchies or dictatorships.

The Democracy Index by Country 2020 has ranked and grouped the countries in the following classifications explained above: [4]

Full Democracy   - 23

Flawed Democracy   - 52

Hybrid Regime   - 35

Authoritarian   - 57

Of the 167 countries ranked, only 23 are truly democratic nations. There is no full democracy in the remaining 144 countries. The political condition of the 29 countries not ranked can be guessed. Among the categories of countries, the largest group is 'authoritarian'. According to

Funds for Peace's Fragile State Index 2020, of the 178 countries ranked, 62 only are stable. List of Fragile and Conflict-affected situations (FCS) released recently (FY21) by the World Bank Group (WBG) shows that there are 17 conflict affected countries and 22 socially fragile nations. The above situation confirms that about a quarter of the world nations is not ruled by legitimate governments and only about 13% of them is fully democratic. In such a frail world political condition, the democracy based western political philosophies can serve academic purpose only.

Emerging Political Issues

According to Richard J. Arneson, political problems of the present day are interestingly unique, giving rise to theoretical questions that earlier political philosophers did not have to confront. Two contrasting features of the world in the early 21st century, for example, are the increasing integration of national political and economic systems and the continuing gross inequality of wealth between developed and less-developed, or underdeveloped, countries. Both features suggest the desirability, even the necessity, of developing political philosophy in order to make it more applicable in a global context. Such considerations have led the Indian economist Amartya Sen and the American philosopher Martha Nussbaum to explore the possibility of a "global" theory of justice. Nussbaum has argued that every inhabitant of the globe is entitled to the conditions that enable one to attain a decent and objectively worthwhile and valuable quality of life. Other philosophers have argued for the justice or necessity of a single world government or of forms of government other than the nation-state. The advent of nuclear weapons in the mid-20th century increased the interest in traditional just-war theory, especially as it applies to the issue of the proportional use of force. Later in the century, the proliferation not only of nuclear but also of chemical and biological weapons made the application of just-war theory to the contemporary scene seem all the more urgent. In the view of some thinkers, the increasing menace of international terrorism in the early 21st century has changed the scope and conditions of justly prosecuted wars, though others vehemently disagree. The nature of terrorism has itself become a philosophically debated question, some philosophers going so far as to assert that terrorism is justified in some real-world circumstances. The adoption by many countries of liberal-democratic forms of government in the second half of the 20th century, especially after the fall of the Soviet and eastern European communism in 1989–91, led some political theorists to speculate that the liberal model of government has been vindicated by history or even (as Francis Fukuyama asserted) that it represents the "end" of history—the culmination of the millennia-long political development of humankind. Be that as it may, many theorists, confident of the basic viability of liberalism, have taken the view that the most important questions of political theory have been settled in liberalism's favour, and all that remains is to work out the details. [5]

On the contrary, the Global Financial Crisis of 2007–2008, perceived economic imbalance due to globalization, sudden large-scale immigration to Europe due to internal armed conflicts in a few states of Middle East, the unexpected spurt in international terrorism, and the so-called identity crisis in developed countries have shaken the above confidence of liberalists and these factors have led to the rise of populism questioning the very relevance of liberalism.

UNIFIED POLITICAL THEORY

American political scientist, Francis Fukuyama who asserted the end of political history on the success of liberalism has now altered his stand and justifies identity politics saying, "What I said back then [1992] is that one of the problems with modern democracy is that it provides peace and prosperity but people want more than that... liberal democracies don't even try to define what a good life is, it's left up to individuals, who feel alienated, without purpose, and that's why joining these identity groups gives them some sense of community." [6] In the present political scenario, the earlier view of Fukuyama on the end of western political history is reasonably acceptable; but his later view needs to be interpreted as the reflection of the present urgency for a fresh approach to political philosophy turning away from the pathway of current western political thoughts. Because, the western political theories cannot afford to keep on discussing 'happiness' 'satisfaction' 'identity' and 'good life' of materially gratified people, when hunger kills around 9 million people every year and 10% of the world population lives in extreme poverty conditions.

U-Turn in the Road of Western Political Philosophy

From the period of Industrial Revolution in Europe, which shifted the concept of wealth from land to capital, the western political philosophy slowly started shifting its focus from the political relationship to economic relationship between individual and state. Following this trend, in the mid-nineteenth century, Marxism was developed, and socialism in general gained increasing popular support, mostly from urban working class. After the World War I, communist and socialist states came into being. In the post-World War II period, innovative advancements made in science and technology suddenly pushed the volume of production and reduced the cost of goods. The business houses of industrialized nations sought new markets of other countries to sell their mass-produced goods and at the same time insisted lesser regulation on their business by the state. In response to this demand, political and economic liberalism gained currency and the world started to realize the huge economic benefits of current version of globalization. This led to the end of 'Cold War' and fall of communism from 1989 and integration of China and similar protectionist countries with global economy. Many countries adopted liberal democratic form of governments. As the result of globalization, about one billion people were lifted from extreme poverty since 1990. Global wealth and average per capita income of world population also increased considerably. Liberalism and the free market created a euphoria among international community. Formation of the European Union (EU) was the peak of achievement of liberal internationalism. Therefore, as stated by Fukuyama in 1992, that was the end of the road for western political philosophy. But, while crossing the 2007–2008 global financial crisis, the above road took a sudden sharp U-turn reversing the cumulative ideological benefits of western political philosophies. After the global financial crisis, the US and European nations grew sceptical about liberalism and globalization and they started to shift their political ideologies from international liberalism to protectionism. Some political leaders of these countries believe that with further globalization, other nations would get stronger politically and economically and hence they will have to lose their traditional image and prominence in the world order. Playing to the gallery of 'common people', they propagate that globalization and immigration would affect their economic interests. The recent rise of right-wing populism in the US and Europe which opposes globalization and immigration reversing their self-nurtured policy of liberal internationalism, and the final decision of the UK on the BREXIT demonstrate the above U-turn in the direction of western political philosophy. In the long political history of the world, political theories have always progressed in a linear way, towards enhancing the individual's quality of life by safeguarding their rights, liberties, freedoms, safety and security, sometimes even underplaying or ignoring the importance of state. Revolutions were made based on these philosophies to free the people from the sufferings of despotic rulers and gain political and economic justice. At no point in time, there was a such a sudden reversal in the evolution or application of political philosophy, as has happened recently. Whenever, there were deviation from the internationally approved political framework, like Naziism, fascism and oppressive totalitarianism, local and international communities have corrected such aberrations, and political philosophies supporting these trends including communism and anarchism failed to progress. For the first time in the history of the political philosophy, the current populist ideologies have been developed for protecting and leveraging the interest of a section of society, unmindful of the concerns of people who belong to other groups or the collective interest of the society or nation. This new trend of political ideology constructed on some flimsy and untenable grounds of populist demands with the sole intension of polarizing societies for electoral gains, totally deviating from the existing tenets of political theories cannot be considered as the extension of the mature and seasoned western political philosophy. The only western political concept the populists rely on is nationalism. But the neo-nationalistic policies of populists are totally opposite to the principles of classic nationalism. The classic nationalism attempted to organize people on some shared common identity to form a nation state with the majority of members of that group and after formation of the nation state, it always maintained the social cohesion and national pride. On the contrary, the present populist ideology tries to form a group with common people supporting some conservative and non-progressive ideas (with which identity is claimed) with the aim to polarize and divide the society of a nation state ignoring the national and global public interest. They call this new ideology as neo-nationalism and the people who do not support this group are ironically called 'anti-nationals'. Human rights of such branded anti-nationals are suppressed with violence and misuse of law. Paradoxically, the political leaders supporting neo-nationalistic ideals undermining the collective interest of their nation take pride in claiming themselves as "nationalists". This happens in the world's oldest democracy, the USA and the world's largest democracy, India.

The best practical illustrations to the reversal and U-turn taken in the pathway of western political philosophy is the demolition of Berlin Wall in 1989 and the recent erection of Trump Wall between the US and Mexico. The traditionally ethical and rational political philosophies of the past cannot accommodate or tackle the new ideologies of populism, as they are constructed on false and concocted facts and ideas, re-writing history and superimposing realities with the support of its irrational and imprudent narratives and arguments. As the populist ideologies form a new genre, totally different from and contradictory to the conventional principles and inclusive objectives of western political philosophy, a new kind of political theory needs to be evolved to counter them with fresh and powerful narratives and perspective developed in the background of the latest political, economic and social developments around the world.

Need for Global Approach

So far, all political theories analysed the issues of origin, structure, purpose, sovereignty and legitimacy of state, various forms of governments and their mandatory functions, relationship between the state and its citizens etc. Generally, all philosophies are state-centric; few like utilitarian and social contract theories lay down general principles, and philosophies like Marxism and Anarchism question the authority and existence of the state. Concepts like internationalism and transnationalism describe the relationship among states. But till now, no philosophy has prescribed the political relationship between a state and the international community with reference to its global collective responsibilities and obligations towards its common good. In this globalized world, all states have become interconnected and interdependent. People are also getting increasingly connected worldwide, politically, economically, socially and culturally with growing commercial and social interactions that happen digitally and physically with the help of advanced digital and communication technologies and transportation facilities. Now, national borders are disappearing and different cultures of the world are getting assimilated in virtual and real landscapes. Similarly, any critical problem of a state has international impact directly or indirectly. Economic, social and cultural spheres of many conservative states are expanding rapidly and turning global. In this fast-evolving global environment, current political theories cannot remain confined to the policies of state alone, as in the case of western political philosophies. Future political philosophies will have to see the comprehensive picture of the political, economic and social system at global level, with its nuances, dynamics and interplays vis-à-vis state's domestic policies and evolve inclusive political theories to ensure a harmonious and sustainable world.

Unity in Diversity of States – Need of the Hour

In order to consolidate, conserve and carry forward the human achievements made so far, there is an urgent need to address the historically persistent problems like poverty and armed conflicts and the newly emerging challenges like increasing inequality, climate change, and international terrorism. In the past, all western political philosophies revolved around the physical, psychological, political and social perspective of human beings in relation to different socio-political institutions and different forms of governments that existed at the time of their evolution. However, in the post WW II and colonial period, modern Westphalian nation state system has become the standardized political structure of governance and over the years, governments of various nature and constitutions have also been stabilized in every state. With this development, without giving room for any further speculation by political philosophers on the form and structure of the political institution of governance, the modern nation state system has become the standardized political unit and the only internationally approved functional machinery to address all political, economic, social, environmental and human development issues of its citizens. In result, an individual's social, economic and political status and aspirations are now solely guided by the state, wherein he/she lives in.

Lifestyle of every person is groomed by the social genome inherited by him/her and the politico-socio-economic environment in which he/she grows. The DNA structure of this social genome is made up of the factors like his/her country of birth, ethnicity, race, tribe, religion, religious sect, caste, community and parents, which a new born baby cannot choose. This inherited genome makes a big difference in the quality of life of every person from birth. Everyone knows that the prospects of lifestyle of children born in Denmark and Somalia are totally different. Still intriguing situation is like this: Assume that a Somalian couple of specific ethnicity, race, tribe, religion, religious sect and community have migrated to Denmark and become the citizens of Denmark by the legal process of naturalisation and give birth to a child in Denmark. This child would naturally acquire the citizenship of Denmark. At the same time, another child is born to a Somalian couple living in Somalia belonging to exactly the same set of social background of the couple migrated to Denmark. Obviously, the lifestyle of this child would be much different from the child born in Denmark, despite the fact that both the children inherited the same social DNA. The only difference between these two children is their country of birth. This is where, the importance of the state in playing crucial role in human development can be appreciated. Therefore, if any community is not able to achieve the desired level of human development, the state to which the community belongs alone is responsible for such backwardness. If this logic is extended internationally, without the cooperation, will and participation of every state, the life-threatening global risks cannot be mitigated and consequently even the very important SDGs like alleviation of poverty and reduction of inequality cannot be achieved. Since the risks are interlinked and global in nature, it is imperative that all the states should coordinate and cooperate in the efforts to address them collectively, irrespective of their divergent political constitutions and policies. But unfortunately, as discussed earlier, many states are presently suffering from congenital and behavioural disorders unable to fulfil their domestic and international obligations and therefore they are not in a position to take part in the concerted efforts of states even with the minimum objective of addressing the principal global risks.

States from Switzerland to Saudi Arabia, Norway to North Korea and Singapore to Syria are run by governments with different hues and colours with different forms of state political structures with varying degree of legitimacy and citizens' political rights and freedoms. Similarly, citizens' immediate demand from the government also varies from state to state. When alleviation of poverty is the dire public need in one part of the world, LGBTQ rights may be a public demand in other part of the world and when call for ethnic and religious rights may be a crucial political issue in one state, price reduction and job creation may be the key demands in some other state. Therefore, the priority of public expectations from the government varies from state to state and from time to time depending on the existing politico-socio-economic conditions. Normally, political theories evolve reflecting the changing structure and behaviour of economy and society of the time, like from capitalism to socialism. Similarly, a state also keeps altering its political approach reflecting the changing aspirations of its rulers and citizens. For example, the USA and European countries which championed the cause of international liberal order are now opposing globalization. Once isolationist China has now turned out to be the biggest beneficiary of globalization and canvass for free market economy. Mere change in government of a state also alter its political philosophy. E.g., the policy changes in the USA after Trump. In such a divergent and dynamic conditions of the world politics and economy, there cannot be a uniform political theory applicable to all states, as aspired by western political philosophy. Even within a state, changing governments and constantly evolving/changing policies do not allow to make a social contract of any nature for the delivery of an identified set of essential goods and services to all or the majority or the most deserving group of the population in a state to improve the quality of life of citizens to certain level. Therefore, in this varied and shifting political domain, it is not possible to evolve a single political theory either for a state or for all states for all times. At the same time, the UN and most of the leading world economists and political scientists and more particularly, the present youth agree on the fact that addressing life threatening global risks and creating conditions of harmonious and sustainable international political and economic order is the foremost obligation of all states for the sake of survival of the human civilization. In view of this urgency, it has become imperative to converge the international political attention to the point of addressing the above issues in a collective manner without any diversion or delay. To meet this urgent need, all states notwithstanding their different static or changing political constitutions and government's policies and practices should necessarily give top priority to the collective efforts of the world community in mitigating the calamitous global risks and in achieving sustainable human development. In short, states as political organs have become stabilized and powerful over the past century with different identities and diverse characters; but their survival is dependent on their collective, concerted and synchronized efforts to address the global risks that are threating to end the life on the Earth and break the world order. Hence unity in diversity among states to address the global risks has become the need of the hour for all states.

Unified Political Theory

From the earlier discussions, the following conclusions are made:

- The western political philosophies failed to consider and address human development issues at global level prevalent in the form of extreme poverty and armed conflicts.

- They did not have the opportunity of addressing the dangerously emerging global risks like climate change, sharply and widely increasing economic inequality and international terrorism.

- The above continuing and emerging global risks are perceived as serious threat to human development, international peace, order and stability with their cataclysmic universal implications.

- States with different political structures and different forms of governments have been stabilized with the approval of the UN and international community. Hence the state has become the key political instrument in resolving the above crucial problems domestically and globally.

- Congenital and behavioural disorders of some states disable them from focusing on these critical global risks and such states are slowly becoming the spreaders of different risks too across the world.

- The UN, many countries and NGOs involved in human development activities, and majority of academicians and intellectuals agree on the urgency in addressing the above major global risks to save the planet Earth and human civilization.

In the light of the above findings, it has become imperative for all states to address the set of primary global risks locally as well as globally. Every state follows its own policies which may or may not cover these global risks. As discussed already, there is no political theory to address global common good. Therefore, it has become inevitable to evolve a **Unified Political Theory** now to address these risks at global as well as state level without any incongruity. Unified Field Theory of particle physics attempts to evolve a theory to describe all fundamental forces and the relationships between elementary particles in terms of a single theoretical framework. But this theory is yet to be evolved, as it involves study of natural fields and forces which continue to remain challenging to physicists. But in political system, human decisions are involved which are very much manageable. Our aim is to identify a set of essential global objectives and ensure that all the states irrespective of their nature of constitution and form of government adopt them as their own and wilfully take action to achieve the objectives within the state and worldwide, following the international guidelines if any laid down for this purpose, so that the pernicious global risks can be addressed successfully without any discord. The proposed **Unified Political Theory** facilitates this integration and coordination of state policies by prescribing the following simple set of political objects that should be acceptable to all states, locally and universally. Since the functions of all states domestically and internationally should conform to the operational fields of the following objectives, this doctrine is termed as **"Unified Political Theory"**.

1. Safeguarding the biosphere from the catastrophic damages of climate change.

2. Providing basic conditions required for everyone in the world to acquire one's capability by adulthood that enables one to function independently in society.

3. Maintaining a peaceful, harmonious and sustainable world order.

In modern terminology, with some of its faulty programming (failure to consider state legitimacy and poverty), affliction of new bugs (pseudo nationalism and national populism) and the need to add new functionalities (to address climate change, inequalities and transnational terrorism), the current version of western political philosophy has become unserviceable. Consequently, it needs to be upgraded and a new version has to launched satisfying the present basic expectations of all stakeholders and users of the global community. The proposed new version is called Unified Political Theory. The progress made in the above objectives would gradually empower the citizens of all the states with necessary political, economic and social rights, freedoms and liberties enunciated in the western political philosophies. Therefore, the proposed new version will continue to serve the functions of the earlier version too for the public. These political objectives may be altered from time to time in response to the urgent global demands.

INSIGHTISM – INTRODUCTION

Knowledge is the accumulation of facts and data that we have learned about or experienced. It is being aware of something, and having information. Knowledge is really about facts and ideas that we acquire through study, research, investigation, observation, or experience. Wisdom is the ability to discern and judge which aspects of that knowledge are true, right, lasting, and applicable to our life. It's the ability to apply that knowledge to the greater scheme of life. It's also deeper; knowing the meaning or reason; about knowing why something is, and what it means to your life. Insight is the deepest level of knowing and the most meaningful to our life. Insight is a deeper and clearer perception of life, of knowledge, of wisdom. It's grasping the underlying nature of knowledge, and the essence of wisdom. Insight is a truer understanding of our life and the bigger picture of how things intertwine. In a nutshell: If knowledge is information, wisdom is the understanding and application of that knowledge and insight is the awareness of the underlying essence of a truth. [7]

Ignorance is the lack of knowledge, information, education and awareness. American Nobel laureate in Physics David J. Gross opines that many of the major problems in today's world such as racism, bigotry, fanaticism of terror and threat to the environment are caused by the sheer ignorance of the people. He says, "There are many problems and dangers that we all face: the massive inequalities that exist in and among the nations, persistence of useless war and violence, the danger of fanaticism of terror, the threats to the environment and to the health of our planet.....The cause of many of these problems is sheer ignorance - the ignorance of science that could solve many of the world's problems, the ignorance of basic facts such as all of us had a single mother only a few thousand generations ago, makes racism and bigotry still possible while the ignorance of other cultures promote fanatical nationalism. As the possessor of knowledge of the 21st century, one should take the responsibility to strive to dispel this ignorance," [8]

Historically, whenever the human civilization had suffered from the illness of ignorance, conservative myths, irrational beliefs, superstitions etc., this kind of treatment with knowledge, wisdom and insight had cured such diseases. Periods of such all-round treatment given to society in Europe are called the Renaissance Era and the Age of Enlightenment. Such knowledge treatments would have taken place in many other countries of different continents also at different periods that would not have been recorded and highlighted in the history, as in the case of Europe. China, India and Mesopotamia were great repository of knowledge from ancient period and many reformist movements had taken place with dissemination of knowledge in these regions. Social reformers of all countries and communities have resorted to this kind of knowledge treatment only to break the then prevalent regressive and socially harmful customs and practices. Mahatma Gandhi, Nelson Mandela and Martin Luther King Jr. applied this methodology to succeed in their missions. Therefore, knowledge treatment is a time-tested curative practice to remedy the social evils and political ignorance to support the healthy growth of human civilization.

According to Mischa Hildebrand, a knowledge activist, complexity is a big challenge for humans. No matter how educated we are, no matter how much we have learned in the past, we can never know everything.

We will always look through our own, personal window frame at the big picture of the universe. In order to see as much of this picture as possible and to make the best decisions as a society, it is imperative for us to put all the individual frames together by employing a division of expertise, to divide and conquer complexity together. If we want to ensure the survival of our species in the long-run and sustain a flourishing society, we need to find a way to make political decisions based on our collective wisdom and knowledge, not on the emotions and alleged intelligence of the masses. Smart decisions require the consideration of all facts and relations, no matter how complex or dry they might appear. The conjunction of democracy and the Internet prevents us from making good decisions as a society because it inherently puts those people in power who present the simplest and most emotionalizing answers for our problems, rather than smart people with thought-through solutions. Our current political system cannot succeed alongside the Internet. It is time for us to rethink. We need to figure out if and how democracy can be modified to yield good political decisions for us, to benefit our society in the 21st century. If we do not succeed in adjusting our political system for modern times, we will fall victim to our own collective stupidity. [9]

As discussed earlier, despite having the capacity to effectively address the global risks, they remain stubborn to get resolved, which in turn impair the human development. This peculiar condition shows that something is blocking the potential of the capacity and someone is interested in keeping the problems purposely alive. These blocks cannot be physical, as it can be identified easily. Hence it should be mental, emotional and managerial. This kind of non-physical blocks can be broken and cleared only with the help of knowledge, wisdom and insight by sensitizing the governments and the public about such blocks and creating awareness on the urgency of finding solutions to the major global risks. This process will expose the vested interests responsible for the blocks and activate the public opinion in favour of finding quick solutions. With the availability of abundant knowledge and information in all spheres of life in today's digital age, it is possible to analyse such inputs and find proper solution to every human problem including global risks.

Knowledge and information lead to clarity to understand problems. This understanding enables analysis of the problems leading to wisdom. This wisdom creates awareness and insight into the problems that lead to ideas for finding solution to the problems. In general, **Insightism** may be defined as an idea of creating awareness with the power of knowledge, wisdom and insight on perilous political, social, economic and environmental issues of the present and future, which are pragmatically and rationally perceived as harmful to the global society. Insightism does not support or incline towards any particular political philosophy. It is neither dogmatic nor normative. It is rather pragmatic and flexible, more particular about the positive outcomes. It is neutral and does not oppose any present political ideologies with its own specific doctrines. It prefers to neutralize the impact of current negative ideologies, by creating awareness about their adverse consequences, inviting public attention towards correct counter theories and arguments. It approaches every problem with independent and impassionate study, assessment and action plan. In short, insightism is procedural and adaptive, and not an independent ideology with an exclusive set of dogmas. It prescribes certain courses to mitigate the long-accumulated burdens of mankind and currently emerging global risks, and provides an alternative to the present helpless and imploding political system.

INSIGHTISM – EXPLAINED

Collective Responsibility for Global Risks

Considering the recent formation of nation states compared to the very long history of mankind and the natural principle of collective ownership of the earth and its natural resources, insightism propounds that all nations and every able adult individual of the world are responsible and accountable for the present catastrophic global risks, notwithstanding their present political, economic and social status and legacies. This stand gets further strengthened by the fact that the impact of these risks is not state specific and it has started to manifest in different ways with different intensities from international terrorism to forest fires and from frequent cyclones to mass transnational forced migration, across the world.

Global risks are not only interlinked to each other, but their impact is felt internationally regardless of their origins. For the present chaotic conditions of fragile and conflict affected countries, so many global factors, including the past colonialism and the present direct or indirect external interference by other state and non-state actors in their internal social and political affairs are said to be responsible. There are evidences to show that many fragile and conflict affected countries have become the breeding ground for extremist organizations and terror groups and international terrorism is exported from there, which is considered as the fast-growing and most dangerous global security threat. Extreme poverty, natural disasters and violence force the people of these countries to migrate to other nations, which many European nations perceive as the newly emerging biggest global risk of this century. Unregulated globalization has led to unprecedented inequality in wealth and income within and between countries. Industrialised countries of the world mainly contribute to global warming which has triggered consequential natural disasters in many countries of the world. All the above problems though originated in some part of the world, lead to safety, security and economic threats at global level. The latest example to the global impact of a major risk is COVID-19 pandemic. Its fast spread across nations indicated how strongly human community is bonded internationally. As far as its political impact is concerned, it triggered tension between the USA and China, the world's most two powerful nations and made the USA to quit the WHO. It has adversely affected the economy of every country of the world without any exception and this economic impact has revealed how intrinsically the production of goods, the service sector and the market are connected globally. At the same time, it also exposed the limitations and absence of effective and interactive health services network among nations. This pandemic has taught a lesson to the world on the importance of facing a global crisis in a collective manner synergising the resources and efforts of all countries of the world to enable to face it without panic and with less damage. It has also demonstrated the assertion of insightism that global risks need global coordination in addressing them.

All the western political philosophies discuss the relationship between a state and its citizens. In this strongly interconnected and interdependent world, insightism attempts to define the relationship of a state and its citizens with the world community. In the present world, a state and its citizens cannot exist and function in isolation. Hence, insightism considers that a state's functions and obligations cannot be restricted to its citizens alone and they have to extend to the global community. Mandatorily, every state has to play its dual role, one for its citizens and another for the global community. So far, no political theory has taken a view on the need for sharing and mitigating the global problems collectively by all states and citizens of the world and prescribed the dual role of the states. International cooperation is different from international sharing of problems. International cooperation may benefit only the states which agree to cooperate on specific issues and this will not address the common global problems. In the present messy conditions of the world, different global problems keep emerging at different places and in different periods across the world, like the present coronavirus pandemic. In the absence of taking collective responsibility of such problems by the world community and concerted effort to address them, we cannot find quick and permanent solutions to these problems. Therefore, insightism makes every country and every citizen of the world responsible for all the present and future global risks, irrespective of the fact whether a country is responsible for or impacted by such global risks or not. Every state has its own duties and responsibilities towards the progress of the human civilization, besides its local obligations which may vary from country to country. Regardless of the capability of participation and the measure of contribution of a country towards the mitigation of global risks, the willingness of it taking responsibility for the risks itself will help to build a consensus on the collective responsibility among nations and synergise the activities of mitigation. The proposed **Unified Political Theory** emphasises the above views.

For the purpose of studying and addressing any global risk, there should be spontaneous and voluntary international cooperation among world community. Insightism suggests that an all-purpose and broad universal framework with due process for intra-state and interstate (regional and global level) interaction and coordination and management protocols should be evolved internationally to manage any global risk effectively with immediate response mechanism. Such framework may be customizable to the requirements of the nature and demands of the impact of a particular risk. This response mechanism may be long term process like in the case of global warming and eradication of poverty or immediate and short term as in the case of natural disasters and pandemics. Such international framework will address all the risks involving long term process with direct and indirect participation of all countries as planned and scheduled. This common framework with customizable and flexible mechanism should automatically facilitate instant response to the sudden impacts of a global risk like natural disaster faced by people at any part of the globe, at any time with nearly available resources and manpower without waiting for orders from the hierarchy of administration. While the impacts like natural disasters and pandemics need immediate short term physical coordination, the long-term efforts like mitigation of global warming needs to be constantly monitored internationally with appropriate dashboard as done now. Insightism wishes to develop a culture among citizens of every state to own the responsibility for all the global risks and be responsive to them in whichever possible way, irrespective of the origin of risk or its area of impact.

Universal Common Good (UCG)

The proposed objectives of the Unified Political Theory and the Collective Responsibility for Global Risks make it obligatory to identify a set of common good which are agreeable to all states that attempt to mitigate the principal global risks collectively at the earliest in the common interest of the global community. Insightism presents this view not on any moral or ethical grounds. It has become indispensable in the interest of safety and continuous progress of human civilization and to maintain a peaceful, harmonious and sustainable world. With the above exigency, insightism prescribes the following **'Universal Common Good' (UCG)** as an obligation for the world community to be discharged in the collective interest of the entire mankind. Without making John Rawls's "thought experiment" and going behind the "veil of ignorance", the following Universal Common Good has been identified in a rational manner to protect the right to life of every individual, which is the basic requirement to claim any other rights and demand any kind of justice. The UCG is procedural in nature and non-excludable.

- Taking climate positive action as planned and agreed internationally.

- Complete eradication of extreme poverty in all forms, everywhere.

- Controlling fast-growing economic inequality within and between countries before reaching the breaking point.

- Moderating and eliminating the causes of large-scale and religious armed conflicts and international terrorism.

Except some populist political parties, religious and social movements, majority of the rational adult population in each state will support the above UCG without any hesitation. The UCG is independent of the nation specific public good and welfare schemes identified by the government of a state and they may overlap on each other. However, in case of dispute between the two, the UCG will take precedence over the state priorities, applying the broader objectives of Unified Political Theory. In future, there should be a strong demand from public and international organizations to include the UCG also in the agenda/programmes/policies of the political parties and governments in every state, irrespective of its nature and form of government. This UCG will become the minimum common political framework of all states independently and collectively to serve the objectives of Unified Political Theory.

Threshold Economic Justice

Insightism does not go into ethical and moral aspects of politics, as they vary from place to place and from time to time. However, applying its principle of Collective Responsibility for Global Risks, it holds the entire world jointly responsible for the prevailing extreme poverty conditions, impacting one in every ten persons of the world. There is no justification of any kind for the death of about 9 million people every year due to hunger and malnutrition when one third of consumable food produced in the world is either lost or wasted. Allowing these pathetic conditions to prevail in this sufficiently well-developed world of fast-growing millionaires and billionaires amounts to committing the greatest economic and social injustice in the history of mankind. In a pragmatic sense, insightism does not expect economic equity or equality among all members of the global society. However, it criticises the discrimination and condemnation of the poor on the basis of their social, economic and capability conditions to a perpetual state of destitution without any scope for their upward social and economic mobility. If the argument that the historical and current faults committed by various international actors are responsible for the present deprived conditions of less developed communities is acceptable, then **corrective justice** demands the rectification of the damage caused to such communities. If the existence of extreme poverty in some pockets of world is perceived as due to failure in the reasonably fair distribution of natural resources of the world among different societies, then **distributive justice** mechanism should be invoked to correct this bias. In either case, the basic canons of justice make the global society obligatory to take necessary action to at least lift the deprived people from their extreme poverty conditions permanently. The above enunciated principles of Unified Political Theory, Collective Responsibility for Global Risks and Universal Common Good do not expect the conventional social and economic justice mechanism to address the risk of extreme poverty, as it is unrealistic in this age of liberalism and free market economy. But it insists for a bare minimum economic justice mechanism to eliminate the global risk of extreme poverty completely and permanently. Insightism describes such limited version of economic justice which enables the extreme poor to break the bondage of poverty as **Threshold Economic Justice.** Transcending societies and states, the Threshold Economic Justice will provide minimum required conditions and opportunities for the vulnerable people regardless of their domicile, to break the cycle of poverty permanently and cross the threshold of extreme poverty. The deliverance under this justice system need not be monetary or commodity benefits and there is also no need to apply the basic principles of justice like equality or equity. The benefit should be by providing necessary minimum conditions and opportunities for the underprivileged people that will make them economically sustainable permanently. Once a person is economically independent, he/she will be able to claim and gain all political and social rights and freedoms.

All states should take appropriate steps in the direction of achieving this Threshold Economic Justice in deprived communities wherever they exist, independently or jointly in association with the UN and its agencies and voluntary human aid organizations. In this process, insightism considers that policies like anti-globalization, anti-immigration and anti-environmentalism which impair the human development of less developed countries should be neutralized. Insightism intends to expose the fallacies of these anti-poor policies, as they tend to disrupt the Threshold Economic Justice mechanism. Further, there should be a concerted effort by the global community to bring the weak and failed states from out of their fragile and conflict conditions, so that they can be part of the activities independently or jointly, in ensuring the Threshold Economic Justice to their communities. The program of achieving Threshold Economic Justice globally should be mandatorily integrated with the policy framework of every government, even if this justice mechanism is already prevailing in a state.

Right to Become a Person

According to the 14th century Italian poet and philosopher Dante Alighieri, the aim of civilization is to actualize human potentialities and to achieve that "fullness of life which comes from the fulfilment of our being." Economist Amartya Sen explains this in his Capability Approach relating to human development as people's well-being depends upon what they are actually capable of doing and being. According to him, the basic question to ask when comparing societies is 'What is each person able to do and be?' – that is, Sen's approach goes beyond the total average well-being in a society, and rather looks at the opportunities available to each person. The process of acquiring the potentialities and capabilities by a person that enables oneself to sustain independently and respectfully in society without anyone's assistance is termed in insightism as **'becoming a person'** capable of doing something and becoming someone in the society. Insightism firmly believes that every person in this world has the basic **'right to become a person'**. Unable to do something and becoming someone in society, a person is socially, economically, politically and psychologically imperfect and a non-entity. Such a deficient person will not be in a position to claim his/her other legal rights, freedoms and liberties. Considering this fundamental and critical requirement in the growth of every person in a society, the right to become a person takes precedence over all other rights except right to life. However, this right cannot be exercised by a person all along his/her life, as it is not a 'right to be a person'. Normally, one can acquire one's capability to function independently in society by way of acquiring sufficient education or skill training by the age of 21–22. Therefore, the right to become a person can be exercised till this age only. Every state cannot afford to support a person throughout one's life to live a dignified life. In all developed and some developing countries, the states have already provided necessary conditions for all to become a person. In some developed nations social security benefits are provided during the entire life of a person. Since all the western political philosophies emerged from such economically developed nations, there was no necessity for them to consider and discuss about this basic human right in their political theories. Presently, this right is mostly denied in less developed and fragile and conflict affected nations and hence it has become imperative to demand for the 'right to become a person'. The UN, its agencies, the World Bank Group and all voluntary human aid agencies should directly or indirectly help the states, where underprivileged communities exist, to provide necessary conditions for their citizens to exercise this right. **Right to Become a Person** is the most essential component of the mechanism to ensure the **Threshold Economic Justice** and the delivery of the **Universal Common Good**,   "Complete eradication of extreme poverty in all forms, everywhere" and to achieve the second objective of the **Unified Political Theory**, "Providing basic conditions required for everyone in the world to acquire one's capability by adulthood that enables one to function independently in society".

Women Development is Sustainable Development

Insightism strongly believes that it is not possible to mitigate all the global risks and achieve the goals of sustainable human development without empowering the women across the world. Had the women been liberated and empowered to the present level at least after the World War II, the world would not be facing this much of poverty, hunger, diseases, inequality and violence, as today. Historically, with the advantage of natural physical power, men dominated women, discriminating them in all walks of life. But even as the importance of brain power grew over the past centuries, the stereotype of men subjugating women in family and society continued, in the name of customs, traditions, religious tenets etc. Even today, in spite of the ongoing strong movements of feminism and women empowerment, majority of women in Asia and Africa continue to suffer the burden of the age-old gender stereotypes of their societies.

The situation is not different in western world too. In the more than 200 years old democracy of the US, a woman president is yet to be elected. For the first time, a woman has occupied the post of the US Vice President in 2021. Throughout most of Western history, women were confined to the domestic sphere, while public life was reserved for men. In medieval Europe, women were denied the right to own property, to study, or to participate in public life. At the end of the 19th century in France, they were still compelled to cover their heads in public, and, in parts of Germany, a husband had the right to sell his wife. Even as late as the early 20th century, women could neither vote nor hold an elective office in Europe and in most of the States of the USA (where several territories and states granted women's suffrage long before the federal government did so). Women were prevented from conducting business without a male representative, be it father, brother, husband, legal agent, or even son. Married women could not exercise control over their own children without the permission of their husbands. Moreover, women had little or no access to education and were barred from most professions. In some parts of the world, such restrictions on women continue even today. [10]

Due to the present active feminist movements, the voice for women empowerment can be heard loudly everywhere. There is demand for political, social and economic empowerment of women. Among them, insightism gives priority to economic empowerment. Once women are empowered economically, it will naturally facilitate gender equality, and empower them in all other walks of life. A recent study shows that women's economic empowerment is the right and smart thing to do. Women's rights are human rights; the human rights case for gender equality is incontrovertible. The human development, economic and business gains from empowering women are substantial. Greater gender equality means a country is associated with better education and health, higher per capita income, faster and more inclusive economic growth, and greater international competitiveness. A widely cited McKinsey Global Institute study suggests that closing gender gaps in labour-force participation rates, part-time versus full-time work and the composition of employment would add 12–25% to global GDP by 2025. Other studies, using a variety of methodologies, find similar potential gains. The business case for promoting gender equality is compelling. A growing body of research documents the various ways where women contribute value to each link of the business value chain, as suppliers, leaders, employees, customers, brand creators and community members. Companies with greater gender equality in their workforce and top management reap a variety of benefits. Such companies are better able to attract and retain female talent, to motivate their female workers, to understand and respond to the needs of female customers, and address complex problems by incorporating more diverse views. Several new studies confirm that companies with more women in top leadership and board positions enjoy higher financial returns. More than 90% of girls worldwide now finish primary school and more women than men are now graduating from college in most regions of the world. Yet, despite these gains, large gender gaps persist in all kinds of work, whether paid or unpaid, formal or informal, public or private, agricultural or entrepreneurial. [11]

Family is the field from which the plant of human capital grows. Society and government play only a supportive role of protecting and nurturing the plant. Without providing nutritious food, heathy environment and education to the children, human resource capacity of the members of the family cannot be enhanced. With her multi-tasking ability and the unconditional love and care for the family, an empowered woman can only spend all her resources for the positive growth of her family members and leverage their capabilities, facilitating fruitful outcomes from them. Resultantly, an empowered woman can only enhance the capability of her family members and such capable family members can only add value to the society and the nation. This kind of back-to-back value addition to the human resources in a less developed country can only ensure its economic and human development growth. However, such a human development is sustainable only if there are no violent conflicts and disastrous impact of climate change damages. With their natural ability for maintaining peace, harmony and cohesion in their family and community and skill for amiable persuasion, empowered women can play an important role in safeguarding the members of their family and community from the process of radicalization of all types and encourage and support the activities of conserving environment. Insightism asserts that without the active participation of empowered women in these efforts, global risks of climate change and armed conflicts cannot be mitigated completely by any other means. Progress made in all other aspects of human development is not possible to be sustained without mitigating these two crucial multidimensional global risks. Therefore, insightism considers that empowered women are more valuable than men from the point of sustainable human development. When one teenage girl, Greta Thunberg could sensitize all big and strong leaders of powerful nations and billions of people of the world on the critical importance of addressing climate change problems, millions of empowered women of different countries can definitely play a pivotal role in reducing global warming and armed conflicts. The recent evidence for the superior women leadership is that from Germany to New Zealand and Denmark to Taiwan, woman heads of states have managed the coronavirus crisis more effectively, compared to their counterparts in the big countries like the US, UK, Brazil and India. Insightism proposes that all future political theories and public economic models should integrate women as valuable contributor to state, society and economy including business and groom them as important decision makers in every field of human activity, including policy decisions of governments.

In an effort to break the gender biased stereotypes persisting in various societies and to tap the vast potential resources from women, particularly the qualities and outcomes that cannot be naturally expected from men, insightism insists to create necessary awareness about women's natural and unique capabilities in the society in general and sensitize the government machinery in particular, by disseminating relevant information with factual and numeric evidences.

UVP OF INSIGHTISM

Of the all the global risks, climate change and religious violence pose the toughest challenge to all. Ironically, right wing populist parties and movements of advanced nations which are mainly responsible for global warming do not accept climate change consequences, in spite of the visible and verifiable evidences produced by the scientists, including NASA. Some people think that the process of reducing global warming would impact the industry which in turn affect their labour interests. Generally, people in industrialized countries are petrified about the economic impact of climate positive action, without realizing the available alternatives and the short-term and long-term threats of climate change. Religion has always remained a sensitive political issue and the spirit of secularism is not strictly followed even in many secular democracies. All religions are being politicised and commercialised for vested interests of politicians and non-state actors. People supporting religious fundamentalism are made to believe that religion advocates violence. Many political movements, parties and governments across the world survive on these well nurtured misbelieves. As long as these false perceptions continue to influence the minds of people, misguided by the populists and religious fundamentalists to serve their own interests, these risks are very difficult to be mitigated. Existing political theories or any other social methodologies do not address these perception issues. It is firmly believed that these illusions in the nature of Plato's shadow of reality can be cleared only by insightism with the light of knowledge, wisdom and insight. Insightism strongly rely on the power and participation of women and youth in the above technique of enlightenment. In the present recognizable market jargon, insightism calls this exclusive approach as its **Unique Value Proposition (UVP).**

7

THERAPY FOR CONGENITAL DISORDER OF STATE

TRANSPARENT GOVERNMENT – TOUCHSTONE OF LEGITIMACY

We have discussed that congenital disorder of state manifests in many fragile and conflict affected countries that are lacking in state legitimacy, displaying the symptoms of converging extreme poverty, diverging inequalities and violent armed conflicts. Insightism assumes that political ignorance of public enhances the power, authority and life of an illegitimate government which encourages it to maintain the status-quo of the deprived conditions of underprivileged communities without much resistance. If this state of affairs persists for long, people are conditioned to live under such government and it gains the legitimacy impliedly, like in the case of present North Korea, Afghanistan and many Sub-Saharan countries. In democracies where elections are held fairly, misjudgement made by public out of ignorance in electing a wrong government can be corrected in the next election. But in other forms of government, this choice of changing the government is difficult to exercise and pollical ignorance of public make the situation still worse.

In pseudo democratic, and authoritarian states, rulers who lack political legitimacy take advantage of this ignorance and artificially create disorderly conditions in the state relying on some pseudo nationalistic elements such as historic background, religion, ethnicity, religious sectarian divisions, culture or any other identity, inciting violence and internal conflicts. These chaotic conditions help the rulers to remain in power as far as possible, with the support of a section of society to which it lends support and thereby claiming legitimacy to their government. The persisting disorder in the society and the focus of the government in managing this disorder, make the state gradually weak. Beyond a point of misgovernance, such states fail totally.

We have already discussed in Chapter-IV about the importance of political legitimacy of a government and how it may be comprehensively assessed and self-enforced. For this purpose of evaluating the legitimacy of a state, complete information and knowledge on the internal and external administrative functioning of the government should be made available to the public. Whatever may be the form and nature of the government, whether it is duly elected or not, insightism insists that the bottom line for its claim of legitimacy should be its transparency. Nowadays, government transparency is used as a means of making public officials accountable and fighting against corruption. But in insightism, going beyond the accountability and corruption factors, transparency is construed as a critical element that reflects on the performance of a government, enabling proper assessment of its output efficiency and thereby judge its claim of legitimacy. It is impossible to make governments of all states to follow true democracy to make them legitimate. But all forms of governments can be made transparent as far as possible facilitating assessment of their legitimacy.

Internal and external assessment of the values and efficiency of a government is possible with its transparent functioning only. Such assessment alone can facilitate dispassionate judgement on the degree of commitment of the government to public good and social justice. This judgement will in turn lead to get an insight into the genuineness of the authority and normative claim of its political legitimacy, whatever be the form of the government. This insight is possible only with a 360° assessment of the of the government by the citizens of the state and international agencies, business organizations, and other state governments transacting with the state, as discussed in Chap-IV. Therefore, rather than the form and nature of a state and its government, its transparency is the primary feature that can actually disclose its political, social and economic agenda and value system. Opaque and partially transparent governments, whatever be their source of power (including democratic) and claim of legitimacy, make proper evaluation of their political legitimacy difficult and therefore have to be construed as not legitimate. Transparent government should be the fundamental and the foremost condition for generating legitimacy among its citizens by the rulers and to ensure orderly, stable, and good governance in the state. Consequently, the demand for transparency in governance should take precedence over all other demands from the citizens, including human rights. Because, without transparent governance, nobody can ensure weather the citizens of a state are accessible to the human and other political, social and legal rights and public good and services claimed to be made available to the public by the state. In result, government's transparency takes precedence over democracy too, and fully democratic countries are already having transparent governments. In a pragmatic sense, insightism prefers to judge a state by its current conduct rather than by its legacy and structural constitution. After all, being transparent does not require any structural or policy change for a government. Any kind of government can afford to be transparent to gain the confidence and approval of its citizens.

In this digital age, running a transparent government is not a difficult task. For any state, running a transparent government is an easy and uncontentious way for generating legitimacy. Political insight, the citizens and outsiders get from the transparent functional behaviour of a government will surely guarantee its legitimacy. Government with lack of legitimacy is bound to lose its right to rule either by legal or revolutionary process at some point in time. The measure of transparency is directly proportional to the actual degree of political legitimacy of a government. Continuous process of assessment and getting insight into the political legitimacy of government will naturally cure the congenital disorder of any state and provide solution to all the shortcomings and internal conflicts of the state due to lack of legitimacy. This insight will also make all governments, with or without inbuilt accountability mechanism, logically responsible and accountable to the public and international community. Consequently, the credibility and economic and political rankings and ratings of such governments would tend to go up. Infusing legitimacy in a state with transparent governance will gradually improve the immune response system of the state against the viruses of radicalization and outside interference that cause violent armed conflicts within the state.

HUMAN DEVELOPMENT – SEN'S CAPABILITY APPROACH

Authors Andriana Conconi and Mariana Viollaz discuss the shifting human development paradigm with reference to poverty and inequality stating that development, poverty and inequality are different although intrinsically connected concepts. Poverty has been traditionally defined using only one monetary dimension – typically, income level or consumption. In this one-dimensional approach, poverty is defined and measured as the percentage of the population whose income level (for instance, the per capita family income or the equivalence adjusted family income) is below certain poverty line or threshold defined in monetary terms.

According to Prof Amartya Sen, poverty is a complex and multidimensional concept which needs to take into consideration people's diverse characteristics and circumstances. The poor generally lack not only income, but education, health, justice, credit and other productive resources, and opportunities. Thus, poverty should be seen as deprivation of capabilities, which then limits the freedoms to achieve something, rather than lowness of income. Sen argues that social evaluation should be based on the extent of the freedoms that people have to further the objectives that they value. Poverty in this framework becomes a 'capability failure'

– people's lack of the capabilities to enjoy key 'beings and doings' that are basic to human life. The concept is inherently multidimensional.

Two consequences arise from conceptualizing poverty as the deprivation of capabilities. The first one is the recognition of a negative association between poverty and human development, and ultimately between poverty and people's well-being. The second is a practical one and entails measurement issues. Conceiving poverty as a multidimensional phenomenon implies several challenges in terms of both information requirements - knowledge (data on several dimensions is now needed in order to calculate a multidimensional poverty measure) and value judgments – insight (the relative importance of the various dimensions needs to be defined).

Traditionally, inequality has been focused on measuring the spread of the distribution of outcome variables, such as level of income, educational achievement, or health status, using well known measures such as the Gini coefficient, the Atkinson index, the Theil index, and percentiles ratios. In Sen's framework, equalizing outcomes should not be a goal, because not all people convert outcomes into well-being in the same way. The relation between outcomes and people's well-being depends on circumstances beyond people's control, such as age, gender, family background and disability. It also depends on social conditions, like health care systems, educational systems, prevalence of crime, and community relationships, among other factors. Thus, the goal should be to equalize the opportunities people have to practice their freedoms, and not the outcomes people obtain. In this framework, inequalities of opportunities are seen as constraints to people's choices and freedoms, impacting negatively on their human development and well-being (UNDP, 2005).

Basically, human development, poverty and inequality are all essentially multidimensional and people-centered concepts. They all focus, although in different ways, on people's capabilities having an ultimate impact on people's well-being. Human development involves expanding the set of capabilities; poverty refers to the deprivation of capabilities, while inequality entails people having different abilities and freedoms to choose.

Development, poverty and inequality are different although intrinsically connected concepts. They are at the heart of Amartya Sen's Capability Approach and the UNDP human development approach, and they all have an impact on people's well-being. Development has been traditionally associated with economic growth. This view was challenged by Sen's Capability Approach which introduced a paradigm shift in the way we understand development. This new development paradigm was constructed on two fundamental changes with respect to the previous approach. Development is now focused on the person as the unit of analysis instead of the economy, and the space in which progress is assessed is made of capabilities and freedoms instead of income. Thus, the basic question to ask when comparing societies is 'What is each person able to do and be?' – that is, Sen's approach goes beyond the total average well-being in a society, and rather looks at the opportunities available to each person. [1]

SELF-POTENTIALISATION AND HUMAN DEVELOPMENT

In the widely differential socio-economic, cultural, educational and technological conditions of the world, the set of capabilities that enable human development will usually vary from country to country and from community to community even within the same country. Similarly, the choices available according to one's capability will also vary. It is for the state to assess the available conditions to create capabilities and choices matching to such capabilities and ensure the availability of minimum conditions for all to acquire some capability and matching choices for their livelihood. This process of a person acquiring capabilities according to his/her ability and merit and exercising the freedom of choice from available opportunities matching to his/her capabilities for making his/her livelihood is defined in insightism as **'Self Potentialisation'**. According to the Cambridge English Dictionary, potential (noun) means "someone's or something's ability to develop, achieve, or succeed". Accordingly, the meaning of "empowering a person to develop, achieve, or succeed according to his ability and merit" is assigned to **potentialisation.**

There is much difference between **'self-potentialisation needs'** and **'self-actualization needs'** of Maslow. Maslow's hierarchy of needs is a motivational theory in psychology comprising a five-tier model of human needs, often depicted as hierarchical levels within a pyramid. Needs lower down in the hierarchy must be satisfied before individuals can attend to needs higher up. From the bottom of the hierarchy upwards, the needs are: physiological, safety, love and belonging, esteem, and self-actualization. Maslow's original five-stage model has been expanded to include cognitive and aesthetic needs and later transcendence needs. Final eight-stage model has the following hierarchy of psychological needs:

1. Biological and physiological needs - air, food, drink, shelter, warmth, sex, sleep, etc.

2. Safety needs - protection from elements, security, order, law, stability, freedom from fear.

3. Love and belongingness needs - friendship, intimacy, trust, and acceptance, receiving and giving affection and love. Affiliating, being part of a group (family, friends, work).

4. Esteem needs - which Maslow classified into two categories: (i) esteem for oneself (dignity, achievement, mastery, independence) and (ii) the desire for reputation or respect from others (e.g., status, prestige).

5. Cognitive needs - knowledge and understanding, curiosity, exploration, need for meaning and predictability.

6. Aesthetic needs - appreciation and search for beauty, balance, form, etc.

7. Self-actualization needs - realizing personal potential, self-fulfillment, seeking personal growth and peak experiences. A desire "to become everything one is capable of becoming" (Maslow, 1987, p. 64).

8. Transcendence needs - A person is motivated by values which transcend beyond the personal self (e.g., mystical experiences and certain experiences with nature, aesthetic experiences, sexual experiences, service to others, the pursuit of science, religious faith, etc.).

The growth of self-actualization (Maslow, 1962) refers to the need for personal growth and discovery that is present throughout a person's life. For Maslow, a person is always 'becoming', and never remains static in these terms. In self-actualization, a person comes to find a meaning to life that is important to him/her. In self-potentialisation, a person comes to find a livelihood that is essential for him/her. But the growth of self potentialisation is restricted to the young age of a person when he/she acquires his/her capabilities to earn a livelihood after achieving the physiological (except sex) and cognitive needs mentioned above. Maslow (1962) believed self-actualization could be measured through the concept of peak experiences. This occurs when a person experiences the world totally for what it is, and there are feelings of euphoria, joy, and wonder. On the contrary, self-potentialisation prepares one to live independently and progress in life according to one's capabilities and choices. When self-potentialisation touches the bottom of happiness at the threshold of life, self-actualization touches the peak of happiness at any point of life. Without attaining self-potentialisation one cannot enjoy the happiness of self-actualization. But all persons who crossed the threshold of self-potentialisation may not reach the point of self-actualization. Accordingly, the hierarchy of **Human Development Needs** proposed by insightism is structured in the following order:

1. Biological and physiological needs - air, nutritious food, safe drinking water, shelter, electricity, health, hygiene, etc.

2. Safety needs - protection from natural disasters, security, stability, freedom from fear.

3. Capability needs – education, knowledge, training, skills, technology, to acquire some useful capability.

4. Freedom needs – sufficient opportunities to exercise freedom of choice to pursue a livelihood, according to one's capability.

5. Self-potentialisation needs - realizing personal potential to become someone recognizable and independent in society and acquiring self-confidence to progress in life with that potential.

The difference between rich and poor income countries is that in rich countries, every citizen of the country is already provided with proper and adequate environment for the development of capabilities from the time of birth and the freedom of choice to make from wide options, to progress in one's career or profession, according to the acquired capabilities, whereas, in poor countries no such environment is provided and no freedom of choice is available. Consequently, people living in deprived conditions in these countries cannot exercise their Right to Become a Person. By claiming up the hierarchy of the above **Human Development Needs**, a person can reach the peak of **Self-Potentialisation** by the age of 21–22 and such a person can surely exercise his **Right to Become a Person.** This right will only can relieve the underprivileged communities from the conditions of helplessness permanently and bring them from out of the vicious cycle of poverty. Enabling such capabilities with sufficient knowledge, skills and training and providing reasonable choices to progress in one's life with clear insight are the goals in the process of self-potentialisation. The scope and strength of self-potentialisation of a person will answer the question 'What is each person able to do and be?' pertains to Sen's Capability Approach.

Since self-potentialisation is possible to be achieved with required knowledge and skills, the process of alleviating complex multidimensional poverty and reducing wide range of inequalities has been made simple and one dimensional, i.e., providing necessary conditions for the youth in poverty to access sufficient knowledge, information, technology, skills and training without any discrimination. By self-potentialisation only, it is possible to ensure **Threshold Economic Justice** for all living in deprived communities. Self-potentialisation according to one's capacity and merit without any discrimination will create a level playing field in the society and slowly reduce the gap of inequalities. A study report on the poverty in Nigeria states that historically, poverty has been predominantly dealt with as a lack of material resources or an income deprivation issue. Development work has focused on pushing resources to poor communities. Many have criticised the availability of "free money" through international aid, which they say has created a "dependency syndrome", dishonest procurement and white elephant projects. Aid work has also been accused of fostering paternalism rather than partnership. The reality is that poverty is about more than just money. If money alone were the solution, poverty would have ended: more than $50 billion was given as overseas development assistance to Africa in 2017 alone. [2] The above point proves that self potentialisation of a person is the smarter way to alleviate poverty than providing aid materials and money.

DIFFUSION OF KNOWLEDGE AND HUMAN DEVELOPMENT

Economist Thomas Piketty made a study on the history of economic inequality and summarised the two conclusions of his study as follows in his book, Capital in the Twenty-First Century: The first is that one should not be vary of any economic determination in regard to inequalities of wealth and income. The history of distribution of wealth has always been deeply political and it cannot be reduced to purely economic mechanisms.... The history of inequality is shaped by the way economic, social and political actors view what is just and what is not, as well as the relative power of those actors and the collective choices that result. It is the joint product of all relevant actors combined. The second conclusion, which is the heart of the book, is that the dynamics of wealth distribution reveal powerful mechanisms pushing alternately toward convergence and divergence. Furthermore, there is no natural, spontaneous process to prevent destabilizing, inegalitarian forces from prevailing permanently. Consider the mechanisms pushing toward convergence, that is, toward reduction and compression of inequalities. The main forces for convergence are the diffusion of knowledge and investment in training and skills. The law of supply and demand as well as the mobility of capital and labour, which is a variant of that law, may always tend towards convergence as well, but the influence of this economic law is less powerful than the diffusion of knowledge and skill and is frequently ambiguous or contradictory in its implications. Knowledge and skill diffusion are the key to overall productivity growth as well as the reduction of inequality both within and between countries. We see this at present in the advances made by a number of previously poor countries, led by China. These emergent economies are now in the process of catching up with advanced ones. By adopting the modes of production of the rich countries and acquiring comparable to those found elsewhere, the less developed countries have leapt forward in productivity and increased their national income. The technological convergence process may be abetted by open borders for trade, but it is fundamentally a process of the diffusion and sharing of knowledge - the public good par excellence – rather than a market mechanism. [3]

Insightism fully subscribes to the above view and considers this to be an authentication of Sen's Capability Approach. The above findings of Piketty also support the importance of knowledge and its power to drive the human development, as asserted by insightism.

HUMAN RESOURCES CAN PUSH HUMAN DEVELOPMENT – EVIDENCE

The number of people in extreme poverty has fallen from nearly 1.9 billion in 1990 to about 650 million in 2018, in the world. Poverty was not concentrated in Africa until recently. In 1990 more than a billion of the extremely poor lived in China and India alone. Since then, those economies have grown faster than many of the richest countries in the world and did much to a reduction of global inequality. The concentration of the world's poorest shifted from East Asia in the 1990s to South Asia in the following decade. Now it has shifted to Sub-Saharan Africa. The projections suggest the geographic concentration of extreme poverty is likely to continue. According to the World Bank forecasts 87% of the world's poorest are expected to live in Sub-Saharan Africa in 2030 if economic growth follows the trajectory over the recent past.

In the process of eliminating poverty, China pulled out 700 million people from extreme poverty and Indian achievement was 170 million. Of the total of 1.25 billion people liberated from the clutches of extreme poverty globally since 1990, China and India alone account for 870 million people (70%). Chinese President Xi Jinping declared in February 2021 that China has scored a "complete victory" in its fight against poverty by lifting over 770 million people out of it in the last four decades. According to him, China has now achieved the SDG No. 1, eradication of poverty completely well before the target year of 2030. Everyone is aware of the fact that both China and India have huge population. Opening up of the economies of these countries in 1990s, assisted by the empowerment of the population with education and appropriate skill sets engineered the globally fastest economic growth of these countries in the last three decades. While China could capture the international market in goods, India became the global leader in IT services. This human resource development (capabilities) coupled with their global integration (opportunities) helped self potentialisation of large number of youths of these nations that resulted in huge progress in poverty alleviation, without much external assistance. These facts clearly indicate that the contribution of human resources to economic development of a country is more valuable than infusion of capital and investment. The less developed countries of Sub-Saharan Africa continue to suffer from the increasing poverty levels as they fail to follow the Chinese and Indian model of building human capital. Mere human development programmes in the form of various aid initiatives, without empowering the youth with proper education and skill development would not eradicate the poverty permanently and pull out these countries from the present fragile and conflict affected situations. Behaviour of economic growth globally and the progress made in human development in different countries in the past three decades have taught an important lesson that human resource matters in the wealth development of a nation, and self-potentialisation of youth will tend to make an under/less developed country strong economically, eradicate poverty permanently without outside support, and reduce the gap in inequalities.

DUAL APPROACH TO HUMAN DEVELOPMENT PROGRAMMES

Sen's Capability Approach, Piketty's findings on the importance of diffusion of knowledge and skill in increasing the productivity and reducing the gap in inequality and the above discussed evidence on the role of human resources in the fast growth of human development clearly support the view of insightism that self-potentialisation of the youth of a country with required knowledge and skills is likely to eradicate poverty and reduce inequality among the people of the country and increase its productivity and national wealth. Taking a comprehensive view of the above points, insightism proposes the following **Dual Approach to Human Development Programmes.**

The conventional programmes followed by the UNDP to enhance all the parameters of human development from health to education independently and collectively for decades have not yielded the desired result. The huge reduction in extreme poverty in the past three decades was mainly possible with the integration of China and India with globalization process and their improvement in human resources. Though Sen's approach is adopted to assess the human development score by the UNDP, Sen's Capability Approach is not fully transferred in its development programmes. Alternatively, a dual approach to human development activities in less developed countries is proposed for eradication of abject poverty and debilitating inequality. As per this dual approach, from one side, the human development programmes will facilitate the youth to reach their self potentialisation limit successfully. In this process, the state and external agencies that run the programmes of human development should focus their attention mainly on the youth living in extremely poor communities up to the age of 21–22. The minimum required lifestyle for their education up to tertiary level or acquiring some technical skills and training to reach employable level should be ensured with sufficient infrastructure, qualified educators and trainers and required study tools. This minimum lifestyle entails nutritious food, safe drinking water, electricity, hygienic living space, healthcare, digital technology like broadband and peaceful environment. To enable to create the above conditions and to reduce the cost involved in the maintenance of other members of the family on par with the youth under the programme, the identified children of the age 5 and above may be segregated from their families and groomed in distinct locations till they reach the self potentialisation limit without the hindrance and disturbing influence of the family and the community. It should be ensured that essential infrastructure is available and allotment of fund is made sufficiently for the above youth programme, on priority. On the other side, the human development programmes may facilitate a decent, healthy and safe sustenance of the rest of the poor population, as in the normal course. This clear division of the programmes with dual approach, one exclusively for the self-potentialisation of the youth and another for the reasonable sustenance and human development of the rest of the poor population will simplify the present comprehensive, but complicated process of human development activities to eradicate the multidimensional poverty.

Self-potentialisation programmes are easily measurable with the evaluation of the performance of the youth in their academic and training programmes which in turn will reflect the output efficacy of the respective development programmes run at different places. Similarly, the utility of the programme is also assessable easily by the percentage of the self-potentialised youth who are employed or self-employed matching to the education/skill acquired. This kind of assessment is very difficult with the human development programmes targeted at all members of the downtrodden community to address their multidimensional poverty. Human development programme executed with the sole objective of enabling self-potentialisation of all the youth belonging to communities of extreme poverty for about 15 years will surely make all the youths qualified for decent jobs or self-employment in their own country or other countries. If the relevant education and training programmes are customized after surveying and matching to the local and foreign job market requirements and the current and future scope for self-employment, the success of the programmes can be assured. One such well-planned programme run in a poor nation for about 15 years covering all youth would certainly make the country permanently free from poverty, improve the wealth of the nation and per capita income and the gap in economic inequality will start closing down. In such a condition, the government need not make further investment in human development programmes and seek aids from international agencies. Self-potentialisation programmes can only equip the youth by providing necessary education and training and make them capable for earning a livelihood. However, programmes run either by the state independently or with the help of human aid agencies cannot on their own create jobs and self-employment opportunities for the youth. Here comes the important role of globalization. States which run self-potentialisation programmes have to tie-up with developed economies and MNCs to educate and train their youth customised for their job requirement either locally or in other countries. The newly created human resources may also be matched with the available natural resources of the state that enable to integrate with the global market and thereby create job opportunities. These efforts should be taken simultaneously with the self-potentialisation programmes, so that the beneficiary youth will be able to exercise their freedom of choice for their career or self-employment immediately after acquiring their capabilities. This action only will make the process of acquiring capability and self-potentialisation complete.

INSIGHTISM – A TOOL TO ERADICATE POVERTY AND REDUCE INEQUALITY

Extreme poverty and expanding inequalities are two of the four primary global risks identified by insightism, which are presently attributable to weak states with inadequate or no political legitimacy. Insightism addresses the issues of poverty and inequalities with reference to human development by making right to become a person as a fundamental right. To enforce this legal notion, insightism has conceptualised the Threshold Economic Justice system, whereby all states are mandated to take appropriate action collectively to provide necessary conditions for all to exercise the right to become a person, particularly in less privileged communities. Self-potentialisation is a process through which one can exercise one's right to become a person. Therefore, **Self Potentialisation** helps the poor to exercise their **Right to Become a Person** by which **Threshold Economic Justice** can be achieved globally. The above three concepts propounded by insightism is sure to alleviate the extreme poverty and dangerously widening inequalities in less developed countries and strengthen their socio-economic conditions. These developments coupled with increasing transparency in governance will tend to offset the fragile and conflict condition of the states and provide much needed political legitimacy to the governments, treating their congenital disorders.

LARGE SCALE AND RELIGIOUS CONFLICTS AND INSIGHTISM

After the end of Cold War, international wars have diminished and intra-state large-scale and religious conflicts increased phenomenally across the world. The rise of neo-nationalistic elements like ethnicity, religion and sectarian divisions in countries with weak governments and short of state legitimacy is the major contributor to these conflicts. Like soap opera, these conflicts prolong for years with new episodes, new actors and new situations. These armed conflicts are responsible for the unerasable conditions of extreme poverty and mass displacement of people in fragile and conflict affected countries of Sub-Saharan and Northern Africa, South Asia and Middle East. Mostly civilians are involved in these conflicts. Warring militia and sometimes state armed forces kill innocent civilians. Children are enrolled in army. Safety and security of women and children are always at great risk in conflict zones. Basic infrastructure of the state is destroyed.

According to an UNDP report of August 2004, war and violent conflict pose one of the most difficult challenges and impediments to human development. Of the 20 poorest countries in the world, most have recently or continually experienced violent conflict. According to the Human Development Report 2002, in the 1990s more than 53 internal conflicts resulted in an estimated 3.6 million deaths; the majority were civilians. Frequently, these wars are accompanied by political, economic, and social transition, natural disasters, and profound pressures arising from globalization, which tend to make them intractable and protracted as well. War today is mostly internal, chronic, extending over long periods of time, often based on identity politics and benefited from globalized forms of financing, which include among others the drug trade, arms trade, the exploitation of natural resources and illegal financial remittances. Preventing the death and suffering of millions from violent conflict and building a sustainable peace is the most urgent challenge for human development today.

The World Bank assessed the conflict situations in this pandemic period till October 2020 and warns that FCV (Fragility, Conflict, and Violence) is a critical development challenge that threatens efforts to end extreme poverty, affecting both low- and middle-income countries. By 2030, up to 2/3 of the world's extreme poor could live in FCV settings. Conflicts also drive 80% of all humanitarian needs. Violent conflict has spiked dramatically since 2010, and the fragility landscape is becoming more complex. Climate change, rising inequality, demographic change, new technologies, illicit financial flows and other global trends may also create fragility risks. Both low- and middle-income countries are affected by fragility and conflict.

Against this background, the COVID-19 pandemic adds even greater stress, threatening to reverse decades of advancements in poverty reduction and development:

- Economic activity in FCV settings is forecast to contract by 4.3 percent in 2020, which is 8 percentage points weaker than earlier projections.

- World Bank estimates show that an additional 18 to 27 million people will be pushed into poverty in 2020 in countries affected by FCV.

- There were 79.5 million forcibly displaced people.

- Of those, 85% are hosted in developing countries.

- Some 77% of refugees have been displaced for at least five years.

- More than two thirds (68%) of all refugees worldwide came from just five countries. [4]

The World Economic Forum reported in February 2019 that religious violence is undergoing a revival. The past decade has witnessed a sharp increase in violent sectarian or religious tensions. These range from Islamic extremists waging global jihad and power struggles between Sunni and Shia Muslims in the Middle East to the persecution of Rohingya in Myanmar and outbreaks of violence between Christians and Muslims across Africa. According to PEW, in 2018 more than a quarter of the world's countries experienced a high incidence of hostilities motivated by religious hatred, mob violence related to religion, terrorism, and harassment of women for violating religious codes. The spike in religious violence is global and affects virtually every religious group. A 2018 Minority Rights Group report indicates that mass killings and other atrocities are increasing in countries both affected and not affected by war alike. While bloody encounters were recorded in over 50 countries, most reported lethal incidents involving minorities were concentrated in Syria, Iraq, Nigeria, India, Myanmar, Pakistan and Bangladesh. Hostilities against Muslims and Jews also increased across Europe, as did threats against Hindus in more than 18 countries. Making matters worse, 55 of the world's 198 countries imposed heightened restrictions on religions, especially Egypt, Russia, India, Indonesia and Turkey. [5]

Rationalization and Irradicalization

From the above discussions it is clear that fragile government with lack of legitimacy (congenital disorder) and pseudo-nationalistic elements like religion, sectarian divisions and ethnicity (behavioural disorder) have their combined and mutually reinforcing effect in keeping the armed conflicts alive in many less developed countries. Insightism has identified the action plan of 'moderating and eliminating the causes of large-scale and religious armed conflicts and international terrorism' as one of the four **Universal Common Good**. It has been explained that the virus of armed conflicts is likely to collapse the entire administrative machinery of the state and threaten the world's peace and security by its infectious spread, if not treated in time. Insightism suggests two kinds of treatments for this viral infection. One is by naturally improving the immune response system of the state by providing a legitimate government, so that such strong government can effectively address all socio-economic factors that are the real causes for the conflict and resolve the tensions with people's support. In Chap-IV, we have discussed about the methodologies of ensuring comprehensive and self-enforceable political legitimacy in states. At the beginning of this chapter, it is explained how the transparency in governance will infuse legitimacy in a state that will gradually improve its immune response system against the viruses of radicalization and outside interference that cause violent armed conflicts.

The second method to treat the virus of armed conflict is by vaccinating the state with the human development activities and giving an insight into the real background and objective of the conflict and thereby exposing the vested interests involved in the conflict. As seen in Chapter-III, Prof. Dr. Matthias Basedau and Author Dr.Bettina Koch have given such insight into the ongoing armed conflicts in Sub-Saharan Africa and the Middle East respectively, where majority of the world's conflicts take place. Insightism insists that this kind of country specific valuable insight needs to be transferred from academic literatures to the public concerned in a lucid manner, by various means supported with relevant facts and evidence. This process of **rationalization** should start with the methodology suggested by the above referred authors. It should study the historical narrative of each conflict in detail to know what were the actual causes of the conflict, how it got morphed as a pseudo nationalistic issue, which event or who triggered the conflict at the beginning, who carries on the conflict now, who are the real beneficiaries of the conflict and what political and socio-economic solutions the leaders of conflict offer to the present problems faced by the public at the end of the conflict. The next step should be to identify the irrelevant and false facts, fake news, concocted messages, photos and videos and irrational and post-truth arguments justifying the radical approach of pseudo nationalists and to expose the weakness, loopholes and irrationality of their arguments and propaganda. Finally, to weaken the pseudo nationalists' campaign for armed conflict, the graphic details of consequences of armed conflicts such as increasing poverty, loss of jobs, business failures, killings of civilians, vulnerable conditions of women and children and the sufferings of forcibly displaced people from conflict zones will have to disseminated among public. People in general should be sensitized on the positive aspects of their core national element. For example, in case of Syria, its very long history of civilization and cultural contribution to the world may be highlighted to rebuild the social cohesion. In the case of religious and sectarian conflicts, it should be explained with evidence from religious scriptures and the life of prophets that all the religions want peace and harmony in the society; no religion supports violence and sectarian divisions are not based on the religious fundamental principles; and there were no violence and conflicts due to such divisions till the recent past. To counter the polarizing and protectionist narratives, it may be emphasised with historical evidences that the natural progress of human civilization is not stoppable or reversible in the globalized world; plural and secular society and interaction and interdependence among societies are inevitable; it has been proved historically that no society or country can exist in isolation; and multiculturalism and multilateralism will only pave way for the fair and balanced societies and the world order.

Such rationalization process may be carried out along with the process of self potentialisation of the youth to achieve optimal benefit. Similarly, this enlightening process may also target women in the course of other human development activities which empower them. The benefits of dual approach to the human development programmes discussed above coupled with the rationalization of youth and women are bound to have combined positive impact on the socio-economic development of the community which is likely to neutralize the negative effects of radicalization of public with pseudo nationalistic elements. This combined strategy of rationalization along with the dual approach to human development activities to root out the causes of armed conflicts is termed as **'irradicalization'**. Irradicalization is not a process to counter radicalization. It is rather a comprehensive methodology of insightism which enlightens as well as empowers the poor simultaneously to distance them slowly from the influence of radicalization and violence. It is a vaccinating technique to treat and totally eliminate the virus of radicalization and extremism from the community and thereby arrest its infectious spread in the form of international terrorism.

Need for Global Plan and Timeline to Reduce Conflicts

Religious extremist groups and terrorist organizations have international network, and funding to these entities are made by certain states and business groups which have political or economic interests in the conflicts. There is no UN sponsored universally approved programme, like in the case of reducing global warming, to defuse the ongoing armed intra-state conflicts. Regional and geopolitical strategic interests of powerful nations, fight among different groups of a state to capture or share power, economic interests of various state and non-state actors from within and outside the state, spearheading network of religious fundamentalism, lobbying of unlawful arms suppliers etc., are certain elements interested in prolonging such armed conflicts. These vested interest groups prevent international consensus and plan of action to end these conflicts. Therefore, it is the duty of all truly religious leaders and voluntary organizations, NGOs involved in peace building, people who belong to the conflict affected nations living in the country and abroad and peace-loving activists of the world to build pressure on the UN and big powers of the world to study, address and end all the intra-state large-scale and religious conflicts with appropriate plan of action within a timeframe. It has become imperative because extreme poverty is getting concentrated in these conflict affected countries and human development programmes are not possible to be implemented in these countries in such tumultuous conditions, and more importantly, forced migration and export of terrorism from these countries pose a big threat to global security.

Insightism prescribes transparency in governance to generate state legitimacy and self-potentialisation of poor in the course of dual approach to human development programme for reducing **poverty and inequalities**. The above processes coupled with rationalization and irradicalization techniques are likely to eliminate the causes of **armed conflicts** in fragile and conflict affected countries. These treatments of insightism are sure to address the above three major global risks by curing the congenital disorder of state.

8

REMEDY FOR BEHAVIOURAL DISORDER OF STATE

URGENT NEED TO ADDRESS THE MENACE OF NATIONALISM

Symptoms of behavioural disorder of state manifest in the form of pseudo nationalism and neo-nationalism (mostly in the form of right-wing populism) throughout the world from less developed countries to super powers of the world. When the pseudo nationalism distracts the human development efforts by keeping the states in fragile and conflict affected situations, the right-wing populism of developed nations is working against the global integration and climate action, blocking the pathways of employment opportunities, income and resources to poor people living in underprivileged communities. Further, this new trend of populism attempts to polarize the society by seeding anger and hatred against a section of society, which mostly is in minority and marginalized to gain support from majority of people of the society for electoral benefits. Therefore, when compared to congenital disorder, the behavioural disorder of state has stronger, wider and dynamic negative impact on the cohesion and harmony of the society and human development.

Author Rana Dasgupta explains the ongoing erosion in the structure of modern nation state system stating that the convulsions in national politics are not confined to the west. Exhaustion, hopelessness, the dwindling effectiveness of old ways: these are the themes of politics all across the world. This is why energetic authoritarian "solutions" are currently so popular: distraction by war (Russia, Turkey); ethno-religious "purification" (India, Hungary, Myanmar); the magnification of presidential powers and the corresponding abandonment of civil rights and the rule of law (China, Rwanda, Venezuela, Thailand, the Philippines and many more). The most momentous development of our era, precisely, is the waning of the nation state: its inability to withstand the countervailing 21st century forces, and its calamitous loss of influence over human circumstance. National political authority is in decline, and, since we do not know any other sort, it feels like the end of the world. This is why a strange brand of apocalyptic nationalism is so widely in vogue. But the current appeal of machismo as political style, the wall-building and xenophobia, the mythology and race theory, the fantastical promises of national restoration – these are not cure, but symptoms of what is slowly revealing itself to all: nation states everywhere are in an advanced state of political and moral decay from which they cannot individually extricate themselves.

He signifies the importance of introducing a fresh political approach as proposed by insightism, stating that on the eve of its centenary, our nation-state system is already in a crisis from which it does not currently possess the capacity to extricate itself. It is time to think how that capacity might be built. We do not yet know what it will look like. But we have learned a lot from the economic and technological phases of globalisation, and we now possess the basic concepts for the next phase: building the politics of our integrated world system. We are confronted, of course, by an enterprise of political imagination as significant as that which produced the great visions of the 18th century – and, with them, the French and American Republics. But we are now in a position to begin. [1]

Political Scientist Florian Bieber concludes his article 'Is Nationalism on the Rise?' noting that there is no panacea for nationalism as long as it is endemic to the global social system. However, there are strategies to reduce its exclusionary and virulent side. As this study suggests, the manifestations of nationalism are manifold, thus the response has to be as well. [2]

RIGHT-WING POPULISM AND HUMAN DEVELOPMENT

Today, the need to address the menace of nationalism is felt strongly worldwide realising its serious impact on social, economic and political order of the world. Presently, right-wing populism is on the rise globally and it opposes globalization, immigration and climate action, which make it difficult to address extreme poverty, growing inequality and natural disasters and therefore directly impede the human development activities. Without clearing these new barriers created by populism, it is not possible to address the mounting challenges of global risks and complete the task of achieving sustainable human development successfully. For these reasons, among different ideologies of neo-nationalism, right wing populism gets more attention.

Measured Globalization

While nationalism artificially created physical, trade and economic barriers between nations, globalization attempts to eliminate such barriers. International movement of goods, services and people in a fast and simple way have brought the world nations and global community closure and more integrated. Diffusion of knowledge and cultures without difficulty across the nations has made the people confident and feel at home in any part of the globe. Overall global wealth and average per capita income of the population has increased everywhere. Economic and business integration among countries has created a competitive global market which is considered beneficial to the business as well as consumers.

Globalization is the word used to describe the growing interdependence of the world's economies, cultures, and populations, brought about by cross-border trade in goods and services, technology, and flow of investment, people, and information. Following centuries of European colonization and trade activity, the first "wave" of globalization was propelled by steamships, railroads, the telegraph, and other breakthroughs, and also by increasing economic cooperation among countries. The globalization trend eventually waned and crashed in the catastrophe of World War I, followed by post-war protectionism, the Great Depression, and World War II. After World War II in the mid-1940s, the United States led efforts to revive international trade and investment under negotiated ground rules, starting a second wave of globalization, which remains ongoing, though buffeted by periodic downturns and mounting political scrutiny. [3]

The International Monetary Fund (IMF) identified four basic aspects of globalization: trade and transactions, capital and investment movements, migration and movement of people, and the dissemination of knowledge. Further, environmental challenges such as global warming, cross-boundary water, air pollution, and over-fishing of the ocean are also linked with globalization. Globalization would not have been possible by mere advancements in technology, communication and transportation, and patronage and participation of liberal democracies. The inclusive and synergised process of globalization has been made possible only with the lifting of iron curtain in Europe, dissolution of the USSR and opening up economy in China and India in the beginning of 1990s. A major international development of globalization was the formation of the European Union with 27 member states to create a single market and to ensure the free movement of people, goods, services and capital within the internal market; enact legislation in justice and home affairs; and maintain common policies on trade, agriculture, fisheries and regional development. Among 26 member states (Schengen Area) passport controls have been abolished. A monetary union is composed of 19 EU member states which use a single euro currency.

Notwithstanding the complex theoretical studies on correlation between globalization and human development, one can say that China is the best and the biggest example to show how the globalization has helped in human development. In 1992, Chinese economic reform program moved into the "socialist market economy" period. The move to open trade culminated in China's admission to the World Trade Organization (WTO) - after much negotiation - in December 2001. In 2000, China scored below the world average score in the Human Development Index (HDI) of the UNDP. Between 2000 and 2010, the HDI score of China galloped from 0.594 to 0.706, surpassing the world average and promoting its classification from Low HD to Medium HD countries. In 2020, its HDI stands at 0.761/1.0, with global ranking at 85, classified under High HD countries. According to the HDI Report 2010, since HDI was introduced in 1990, China is the only country in the world which has moved from the low development to high development classification. In the 15 years from 1990 to 2005, China recorded average per capita growth of 8.7%. Between 1990 and 2005, China's progress accounted for more than three-quarters of global poverty reduction and China became the first developing country to achieve the first Millennium Development Goal (MDG) relating to eradication of poverty ahead of schedule. According to the World Bank, more than 850 million Chinese people have been lifted out of extreme poverty; China's poverty rate fell from 88 percent in 1981 to 0.7 percent in 2015 and in 2021 it is claimed that poverty has been completely eradicated. China's life expectancy at birth has increased from 69 years in 1990 to 76 years in 2018. Its expected years of schooling have increased from 8.8 years to 13.9. China has a Gender Inequality Index (GII) value of 0.163, ranking 39th out of 162 countries in the 2018 index. With continuous increase in grain production for 11 years since 2004, China is able to feed nearly 20% of the world's population with less than 10% of world's cultivated land. Since 2000, China had provided safe drinking water to additional 467 million rural residents and kept the net enrolment rates of both boys and girls at primary-school age above 99%. China has become the second largest economy in the world after the USA. This salutary performance of China in human development was possible only after opening up and integration of its economy with world economy. China, a conservative and authoritarian state took full advantage of the globalization and engineered its human development growth most successfully to prove that global integration is the key for sustainable human development. This was possible without manoeuvring its existing political system. Further its success in economic and human development progress has not hindered any other country's social or economic interests domestically or globally. These facts make us to critically analyse the accusations being made against the globalization, particularly by populist leaders of developed countries.

The irony is that while the liberal democracies like the USA and European nations, which spearheaded the ideology of liberalism, globalization and multiculturalism are turning against the global integration, the communist countries which were protectionists and autocratic have opened up, and are playing important role in the global free market economy. In Europe which experimented some new kind of political and economic order by forming the European Union (EU), liberalism is on the decline and its political landscape is held sway by right-wing nationalists. The UK left the EU in January, 2020. BREXIT is a major shock for the dreamers of more broad and significant international coordination like the EU, in different regions of the world. The USA which historically stood for democracy, capitalism and liberal internationalism and benefitted a lot in terms of growth of wealth due to globalization is now under the wave of right-wing populism.

Prof. Pranab Bardhan says that faced with raging right-wing populism across the world, there has been a tendency among columnists to portray it with a broad brush, blurring important distinctions. It is common, for example, to see fingers pointing at the backlash to globalisation. But if one takes the whole range of rich, middle income, and poor countries across continents, there is certainly no worldwide rebellion against the forces of globalization. A survey across 18 countries, reported in The Economist (19 November 2016), suggests that the majority are quite positive on globalisation in India, Vietnam, the Philippines, Thailand, Malaysia, Denmark, Hong Kong, and so on (if China were included, probably it'd have been in the same list). On the other hand, support for globalisation is low in the US, France, Britain, and Australia - the expected fallout in rich countries from the decline in their century-old domination in international trade and investment. Everywhere there is a struggle to find a niche in the ever-changing global value chain and retrain the workforce in line with the changing demand for skills. Similarly, immigration is a major divisive issue mainly in Europe and the US, while the developing countries lobby for relaxation of immigration restrictions in rich countries. [4] For the people in many developing countries, globalization integrated their business with the world business and finance and helped their economic growth. Only a small minority group of people whose business got affected by global competition and who are reluctant to upgrade their skills and technology to the competitive level are criticizing the globalization.

The right-wing populists usually claim that they represent the interest of an identified group in their country, exclusively. In fact, they are internationalists working in close coordination with big business entities across the world. MNCs, their different confederations/associations and pressure groups supporting them have consciously refrained themselves from vociferously opposing the anti-globalization narratives of right-wing populists in developed and developing countries. Their pretension of working for the common public is also not true. Crony capitalism is openly practiced by governments in many populist democracies. Identifying themselves with one or more right wing civil groups, business lobbyists and pressure groups, the populists are willing to compromise with the common national interests of people. This dubiously polarizing approach of right wing populists confuses people and creates lots of socio-economic tension and sometimes violent conflicts in the society.

From the economic point of view, the major criticism against globalization is that it increases income inequality within the country. But such growing inequality within a developing or less developed country need not always affect the people at the bottom. Let us assume that such a country had a population of 20 million people, of them 3 million were under the poverty line and there were 10 billionaires, before going commercially and economically global. After its integration with global market, the income inequality may increase in two ways. In the first model, the globalization may add further 2 million people under the poverty line and rise the number of billionaires from 10 to 100 in a particular period. Such increase in the gap of inequality would definitely hamper the human development of that country and is deplorable. In the second model, if 2 million people are lifted above the poverty line as the result of globalization and the number of millionaires rose from 10 to 200 and still the gap of inequality would widen and such elevation in the measure of gap in inequality is not harmful to the human development of that country. Globalization has benefitted many developing and less developed countries in the recent decades by the second model only. This model was responsible for driving the engine of human development growth so fast in China and India. That is the reason why, there is no large anti-globalization movements in developing nations. Resultantly, any populist movement against globalization has to be generally considered as anti-poor and anti-human development movement.

Despite its benefits, it is a fact that the globalization has disrupted the status quo of national economy of a few countries. Though, there was an overall growth in the wealth of the world on account of globalization, it did not get distributed evenly among population in a country and among countries. While it is advantageous to certain section of people in a country and for certain nations, it puts certain other set of people and countries at economic disadvantage. In developing countries, disruption of their markets and dominance of MNCs have created a fear of economic instability among the public. In the industrial world, public is concerned about the increased global competition that impacts their wages, labour rights, employment practices and the environment. Angel Gurría, OECD Secretary-General remarks that many factors are fuelling global discontent with our economic and financial systems which, in some cases, is evidenced in a backlash against globalization. Rising protectionism and populism threaten to unravel decades of international co-operation and openness that have lifted more than a billion people out of extreme poverty, fostered cultural diversity, and facilitated the fastest convergence of per capita incomes in history. We must protect the benefits that globalization has brought, while recognising the legitimate concerns of citizens who have been left behind, without jobs, and without the skills they need to get one. [5]

Therefore, there is a need to constantly monitor the unbridled economic globalization which always favours big businesses and at some times impacts the economic interests of few sections of the society. In order to correct these variable conditions, the World Trade Organization (WTO) should continuously study the structural weakness in the international trade and market, and attempt to fine-tune the system to address all the grievances of globalization periodically. The framework and policies of WTO should always put a human face by factoring in human development and climate change issues appropriately. Economic globalization encompasses international flows of capital, investments and financial services too, besides goods, services and intellectual property. But there is no single world organization similar to WTO to regulate and monitor the international flows of capital, investments and financial services exclusively. Absence of such an international body has created many transactional disputes and difficulties, particularly to developing nations, where inward flow of capital and investment is more. Therefore, there is an imperative and urgent need to create a World Financial Organization (WFO) in line with the WTO at the earliest to deal with the modalities of international financial transactions exclusively. Besides regulation, this WFO should study the critical issue of growing economic inequality related to globalization and give its country specific policy recommendations on the implementation of welfare schemes and tax systems to ensure reasonable distribution of income and wealth, enabling to moderate the fast-widening gap of inequality within the country and improve the human development indicators. It may also analyse the economic and financial impact of international trade in goods and services and provide required inputs to the WTO to regulate the uncontrolled and uneconomic participation of countries in global trade that widens the gap of inequality between nations. If the present WTO and the proposed WFO coordinate and complement each other in constantly regulating all international business and financial transactions in a dynamic manner under well-conceived internationally approved norms and guidelines, the unintentional negative impact of globalization can be reduced considerably. Such a measured globalization is expected to remain stable and organically mature that can integrate with all political, social and economic systems of all countries effortlessly.

Coronavirus pandemic has now overtaken the right-wing populists in halting the momentum of globalization. According to the World Economic Forum, the COVID-19 pandemic is now expected to trigger the worst economic downturn since the Great Depression. Many argue that it could undo globalization altogether. Globalization relies on complex links – global value chains (GVCs) – that connect producers across multiple countries. These producers often use highly specialised intermediate goods, or "inputs", produced by only one distant, overseas supplier. COVID-19 has severely disrupted these links. Global supply chains (GVC) are extremely complex, and no sector or country is an island. But GVCs follow the principle of efficiency. They are the result of businesses sourcing the best possible inputs to meet their production needs at the lowest cost – wherever those inputs come from. This is good news for globalization's survival. While efficiency remains the main target, businesses will continue to shop globally. Concerns about an overreliance on complex GVCs are justified in the case of products related to national security, such as medical supplies. Many countries will now ensure that they can produce such goods without relying on imports. Nobody can predict the next crisis. But the most reliable and efficient insurance by far is to build a strong international cooperation network.

Another strong argument in favour of globalization is that as the international network of business, finance, health, education, people and cultures grows wider, stronger and deeper it will make all the countries more interdependent and interconnected inextricably. Consequently, any impact in the safety and security of a country is likely to have global impact affecting the interest of people and economy of other countries too directly or indirectly, which we have witnessed in the recent immigration of people from conflict affected countries of the Middle East to European countries and the spread of coronavirus pandemic and its global economic impact. This trend of inseparable integration will shift the focus of the countries slowly from national safety and security to regional and global safety and security. In these increasingly global networking conditions, isolationist countries like North Korea, Myanmar and Iran need to be restrained from militarisation beyond the level that threatens the international peace. Once this job is done, the countries which are part of the globalization process need not bother much about international balance of power and naturally the present world military expenditure of more than 2 billion US dollars per annum will drastically go down, and the savings may be directed to increase social expenditure towards the human development of underprivileged communities across the world.

Immigration is Good

Immigration is perceived as the newly emerging biggest human crisis of this century and the rallying point for populist leaders. There were sharp reactions from right-wing populist movements of the west particularly against immigration from war torn countries of the Middle East like Syria to European nations. However, research suggests that migration is beneficial both to the receiving and sending countries. According to one study, welfare increases in both types of countries. Welfare impact of observed levels of migration is substantial, at about 5% to 10% for the main receiving countries and about 10% in countries with large incoming remittances. Studies show that the elimination of barriers to migration would have profound effects on world GDP, with estimates of gains ranging between 67–147%.

As per World Bank report on "Moving for Prosperity: Global Migration and Labor Markets", migration is the most effective way to reduce poverty and share prosperity. Some of the biggest gains come from the movement of people between countries. The report argues that migration will be a fundamental feature of the world for the foreseeable future due to continued income and opportunity gaps, differences in demographic profiles, and the rising aspirations of the world's poor and vulnerable. Migrants' incomes increase three to six times when they move from lower- to higher-income countries. The gains for immigrants do not come at the expense of host countries. Farmers in destination countries from New Zealand to New Mexico thrive thanks to the hard work of immigrant workers. Institutions at the technology frontier—from CERN (the European Organization for Nuclear Research) in Geneva to Silicon Valley in California— innovate thanks to the ingenuity of immigrants. Native workers of destination nations also gain as they gravitate away from the occupations that immigrants are willing to perform, because they benefit from the complementary skills that immigrants bring, or because they are consumers of the products and services immigrants provide. Almost every empirical study finds that increased labour mobility leads to large gains for the immigrants and positive overall gains for the destination country.

That creates a puzzle. The compelling economic evidence on the economic gains and social benefits of migration sits awkwardly with stark political opposition to immigration. Respondents to political opinion polls rate the arrival of immigrants in their countries as among their worst fears. Citizens worry about what the migrants and refugees would do to their jobs and wages, welfare programs, schools, and their national identity. Frustrated by the public's disregard of their empirical findings, many economists attribute political opposition to cultural and social factors, including xenophobia.

This Policy Research Report is an attempt to address this tension between the academic research and the public discourse by focusing on the economic evidence. We suggest a labour market–oriented, economically motivated rationale to the political opposition to migration. Global migration patterns lead to high concentrations of immigrants in certain places, industries, and occupations. For example, the top 10 destination countries account for 60 percent of global immigration. In the United States four states host half of all immigrants, and 10 counties host half of the immigrants in these four states. Immigrants are further concentrated in a narrow set of industries and occupations in specific geographic regions. The same pattern repeats itself in almost every major destination country. It is these geographic and labour market concentrations of immigrants that lead to increased anxiety, insecurity, and potentially significant short-term disruptions among the native workers. Furthermore, the positive effects and benefits in the destination labour markets tend to be more diffuse when the costs are more concentrated and easily attributable to immigration.

Understanding (and empathizing with) these legitimate economic concerns is critical to informed and effective policy making. The goal should be to ease the costs of short-term dislocations of native workers and distribute more widely the economic benefits generated by labour mobility. Proactive interventions to ease the pain and share the gain from immigration are essential to avoid draconian restrictions on immigration that will hurt everybody. Ignoring the massive economic gains of immigration would be akin to leaving billions of hundred-dollar bills on the sidewalk.

The concluding findings of the above report are:

1. There is empirical evidence to prove that besides the immigrants and their native countries, the destination countries also gain a lot economically, due to immigration.

2. Immigration also helps the citizens of host nations in enriching their skills and competitiveness in innovation and human resources.

3. The space, density and the nature in the distribution of migrants in the destination countries are not properly understood by the policy makers of the countries.

4. If the policy makers of a host country study and understand these aspects of immigration well and make necessary cost-

effective restructuring of resources and manpower to take optimal advantage of the immigration, the negativity against immigration can be removed. [6]

On the whole, the ongoing immigration is good for both native as well as destination countries. Migration has always remained a natural process for human beings. Prehistoric humans were nomadic and always moved from one place to another in search food. 7000 years ago, homo sapiens started migrating from Africa to various continents slowly. In ancient times, maritime nations such as the city-states of Greece and Phoenicia often established colonies to farm what they believed was uninhabited land. Land suitable for farming was often occupied by migratory 'barbarian tribes' who lived by hunting and gathering. In the middle ages, the decline and collapse of the Roman Empire saw (and was partly caused by) the large-scale movement of people in Eastern Europe and Asia. In West Asia, during Sassanid Empire, some Persians established colonies in Yemen and Oman. The Arabs also established colonies in Northern Africa, Mesopotamia, and the Levant, and remain the dominant majority to this day. The Vikings of Scandinavia also carried out a large-scale colonization. The Vikings are best known as raiders, setting out from their original homelands in Denmark, southern Norway and southern Sweden, to pillage the coastlines of northern Europe. In the Colonial Era, colonialism in this context refers mostly to Western European countries' colonization of lands mainly in the Americas, Africa, Asia and Oceania. The main European countries active in this form of colonization included Spain, Portugal, France, the Kingdom of England (later Great Britain), the Netherlands, and the Kingdom of Prussia (now Germany), and, beginning in the 18th century, the United States. Most of these countries had almost complete power in world trade at some stage in the period from roughly 1500 to 1900. Beginning in the late 19th century, Imperial Japan also engaged in settler colonization, most notably in Hokkaido and Korea. [7] Therefore, migration of people from one continent to others and from one country to other countries, either voluntarily or forcibly is not new in human history. Our national borders and political maps of countries are of recent origin. Without such constant migration of people, the human civilization would not have spread and grown across the world, to some extent uniformly. The foul cry of populists against the immigration undermines the importance of migration in the growth and establishment of human civilization at different parts of the globe and such stand is against the natural human behaviour.

Insightism to Neutralize Anti-Globalization and Anti-Migration Campaigns

We have seen that globalization has played a vital role in uplifting about one billion people from extreme poverty. Global economic integration has enabled neutral distribution of income worldwide, without discriminating on the basis of nationality, race, colour, religion etc, as in the case of politics. It is willing to recognize only one's ability, merit, ideas and innovations without any sort of bias. For example, a school student in India can detect a bug in a google product and provide solution. His work is instantly recognized by the US corporate and he is sufficiently awarded without going into his social and educational background. This natural process of economic globalization has contributed to the human development by eradication of extreme poverty in a huge scale in the past three decades that could not be achieved either by the state specific policies of governments or by the UN and other international aid agencies for many decades. If the globalization is regulated properly and allowed to be operated in a measured manner, the present few grievances against globalization can also be addressed. Similarly, we have seen that there are empirical evidences to prove that immigration is beneficial to the sending as well as receiving countries. The above general discussion itself has proved that the propaganda of right-wing populists against globalization and immigration are untenable. After all, migration is in the human DNA and globalization is an organic process in the growth of human civilization around the world.

In fact, the developed countries from the UK to the USA would not have reached their present commanding economic status without the help of the above natural process of global integration. The USA is a country of immigrants and almost all European countries benefitted a lot from colonization. The MNCs of developed nations cannot survive without the support of global market. Insightism strongly recommends that the UN, the World Bank Group, MNCs and more specifically, the digital giants like Google, Facebook, Twitter, Amazon, WhatsApp etc., which benefit from global integration should periodically bring the above historical facts to the notice of the public supported with factual evidences, data and interesting anecdotes, displaying old and recent photos and videos to encourage further global integration.

Currently, insightism insists that country specific study should be made on the impact of globalization and immigration and the positive results disseminated among the pubic concerned to disprove the false claims of populists on the negative impact of globalization and immigration. Many such area specific studies have already been done to prove the positive outcomes of globalization and immigration with factual evidences and empirical analysis. Wherever, populists are actively opposing globalization and immigration, there should be forceful, convincing and wider spread of information supported with numerical and factual evidences to dispel their false propaganda, using all types of digital and conventional media. This campaign may also highlight the concept of insightism on 'collective responsibility of the world community for global risks' to give an insight into the adverse consequences of such anti-poor policies of populists, which are likely to enhance the dangers of global risks like poverty and inequality particularly in less developed countries. At the same time, if such studies reveal some adverse economic, social and security risks in a specific geographical location or in any community on account of globalization or immigration, they should also be acknowledged and brought to the notice of the government authorities concerned with appropriate recommendation to address the issues. Everyone knows that the natural process of globalization and migration has pushed the growth of human civilization from its origin to the present level. The empty rhetoric of populism cannot withstand the force and momentum in the progress of human civilization. Insightism aims to crystalize, regulate and accelerate the process of seamless and win-win global integration for all, with the help of knowledge, wisdom and insight.

Climate Scepticism and Insightism

The impacts of climate change are felt everywhere, as the global climate is a connected system. Rising sea levels, melting ice, storms, hurricanes and typhoons, heatwaves and droughts, changing eco-systems, reduced food security and rise in pests and diseases are the major impacts of climate change, which we have already started experiencing. People in less developed and developing countries face the impact of climate change severely and frequently, even though they contribute least to greenhouse gases emission. Indigenous and elderly people, people living in coastal communities, women and children of these countries are more vulnerable to the dangerous effects of climate change. According to the UNDP, today over 2 billion people - one third of the global population - are poor or near-poor and face persistent threats to their livelihoods, including from climate change. Estimates indicate that by 2030 more than 100 million people could fall back into extreme poverty due to climate change, while over 200 million people could be displaced due to more frequent and severe climatic disasters. Therefore, climate change is considered as the topmost human development issue.

The impacts of climate change superimpose on the existing vulnerabilities of poor communities. Climate change will further reduce access to drinking water, negatively affect the health of poor people, and will pose a real threat to food security in many countries in Africa, Asia, and Latin America. In some areas where livelihood choices are limited, decreasing crop yields threaten famines, or where loss of landmass in coastal areas is anticipated, migration might be the only solution. The macroeconomic costs of the impacts of climate change are highly uncertain, but very likely have the potential to threaten development in many countries.

Despite the emerging scientific evidences linking climate change impact with various natural disasters across the world, the right-wing populists uniformly and consistently deny such link and oppose environmental activism, taking the help of some biased pseudo scientists, funding agencies, MNCs, NGOs and political action groups. Whenever climate-sceptics have challenged climate scientists' time frames, data and theories, the climate change scientists have re-tested the climate-sceptics' data and claims, and improved their own data and reworked their models and theories. Every time they return with improved results, the climate-sceptics also do the same thing. To date, the ongoing research suggests that the climate change models are better and improving rapidly, but the continued contest demonstrates the living nature of the scientific process. Outside the scientific view of the world, however, ignorance of the facts and of science itself have created a free-for-all. Fringe environmental groups, right-wing internet blogs, politicians of all stripes have spread falsehoods far and wide or distorted the truth to serve their own ends.

Like in the case of immigration, the movements against environmental activism are kept alive by articulated narratives of populists, spreading unscientific and irrelevant facts, data and untenable logic, exploiting the ignorance of the public. The impact of climate change is slowly accumulating and it is not easily reversible. At present, its impact may be manageable by rich countries, and the latent potential of the future threats may be swept under the carpet. But, in the long term, scientists predict that if the issue of climate change is not addressed now, the catastrophic transformation in the behaviour of the nature would not spare any part of the world and the consequences would be unimaginable and uncontrollable by anybody. Many future generations will have to suffer due to this impact.

Richard Calland, Associate Professor in Public Law, University of Cape Town explains that increasingly, there is an understanding that the climate emergency is not an environmental problem. It has grave ecological implications, but it's a human development issue above all. And, it has profound implications for technology and infrastructure, for the world of investment and finance, and for global security. In a complex world facing complex problems, it is seductive for politicians to identify a single culprit (like immigrants) or an evil force (like universal healthcare) to blame for the erosion of society, the economy, and the welfare of the masses. Climate change and its effects are perhaps the epitome of a complex issue of interlinked social, political, and physical forces. That makes it an easy target for this sort of denialism. So, populism ends up denying not just the science of climate change but also the complexity of the entire issue – which is critical for both diagnosing the problem and determining the prognosis and the prescription.

He further adds that 2019 study mapping the climate agendas of right-wing populist parties in Europe contains some revealing evidence: two thirds of right-wing populist members of the European Parliament "regularly vote against climate and energy policy measures". Half of all votes against resolutions on climate and energy in the European Parliament come from right-wing populist party members. Of the 21 right-wing populist parties analysed, seven were found to deny climate change, its anthropogenic causes, and negative consequences. According to estimates based on the World Resources Institute's global greenhouse-gas emissions data, about 30% of global emissions come from countries with populist leaders. At the very moment when global cooperation is essential if climate action is to be effective, many of the leaders of these right-wing populist forces are trying to dismantle or weaken multilateral organisations such as the United Nations or the European Union. These political groups threaten to derail progress on the global response to climate change, and on new thinking about how to rewire the economy in pursuit of a more sustainable world.

He applies the core principle of insightism to counter the climate denialism campaign of populists explaining that as grassroots organisations emerge as a potentially strong, countervailing force, the trick will be to effectively connect these movements to matters of global social justice. They should also be given enough coherence to be effective. Thus, again, it is shifting the lens for the climate crisis away from an environmental preoccupation towards human development and social justice. For example, how can Thunberg and the student strike movement in the global north connect with the 1.6 million children that are displaced in Malawi, Zimbabwe, and Mozambique by cyclones? Such connections need to be made to turn these nascent movements into powerful advocates for climate justice. A first step to responding appropriately – individually and collectively – is understanding that the challenge is multi-dimensional. Only then can a multi-dimensional strategy be executed, across sectors and across national boundaries. But it is likely that the greatest impediment to taking action will not be technological know-how or even raising the money required. Instead, it will be the lack of enough political will, given the obstructionism of right-wing populists in power around the globe. Hence, a political struggle will need to be won. And the fight for climate justice in the face of right-wing populist climate denialism is a titanic one. Trump-like trajectories into the "post-truth" world of climate change denial, charged by the amplifying impact of social media, distract from and obstruct the necessary action. Yet despite its flaws, the digital age presents a huge opportunity to impose a counter-narrative, and for recruiting new activists. People can connect more easily across seas and time zones. Climate denialism can be rebutted and populist rhetoric rebuffed. Protests can be arranged quickly. And the young will do it best, not least because they have the deepest vested interest of all: their future is at stake. [8]

Robert A. Huber, research scholar in political science and writer explains that because of its nature, climate change seems to be an ideal target for populism. It is abstract, elite-driven, temporally and cognitively distant (so we rarely see consequences of climate change in the short-run). Hence, we could expect populists – regardless whether they are left or right – to be sceptic about the whole phenomenon for two reasons. First, existing research by Castanho Silva and colleagues emphasizes that populists embrace conspiracy theories. The above-mentioned key characteristics of climate change invite conspiracy theories, scepticism and denial about the existence of the issue to begin with. Second, climate policy was an elite phenomenon for a long time. Climate policy was mostly discussed in international fora. The public, but also citizen groups, were somewhat excluded and the issue was not salient in the media. This aspect invites criticism that climate change is an elite project. However, for right-wing populists a couple of additional mechanisms are plausible. Existing research suggests that right-wing individuals (and parties) are substantially less enthusiastic about climate and environmental policy. With a focus on the US, Dunlap and McCright suggest that Republicans (as more right-wing actors) support free-markets and thus perceive environmental protection as interference with the free market. This is one potential explanation for why right-wing individuals, tend to oppose climate policy. More specifically, Lockwood argues that right-wing populist voters are often directly affected by these policies. According to his argument, right-wing populist parties represent voters who commonly work in low-skilled manufacturing sectors. In Western Europe, environmental regulation might undermine their company's competitiveness. This threat could lead to wage reduction or in the worst case, job loss. Thus, it might be rational for them to oppose climate policy. All these mechanisms can explain how partisanship and political ideology relate to climate and environmental attitudes. We need to disentangle populism and ideology to understand what drives citizens' attitudes towards climate change.

He also emphasises the methodology of insightism, involving public in the action to counter the anti-climate action campaign of populists. He says that citizens' participation is important not only from the perspective of populism and climate scepticism, but also from a more general climate mitigation perspective. Phenomena such as the Gilets Jaunes (Yellow Vests) movement in France suggest that effective climate policy is futile without citizen inclusion. The Gilets Jaunes are not even against climate policy, per se. However, they want their interests to be represented and considered in the making of climate policies, such as the carbon tax that was imposed and then withdrawn in France due to the pressure from the Gilets Jaunes. There are at least two ways forward. On the one hand, there are economic mechanisms that would allow compensating those that are affected negatively by climate policies. For example, combining progressive income tax cuts with the introduction of a carbon tax could bolster public support for climate policies. More generally, combining different policies might help overcome some obstacles. On the other hand, active citizen inclusion, such as citizens' assemblies on climate change, might help to integrate citizens in the debate. The UK recently started a first citizens' climate assembly, France implemented a similar model to address the Gilets Jaunes protests. It is doubtful whether this will change policy outputs, mainly because technical and complex issues, like climate change, benefit from expert involvement. However, contrary to direct democratic votes on climate policy, citizen assemblies could be one instrument to make climate policy more accessible and acceptable, and thus boost public support to tackle one of the most prolific challenges to liberal democracy in the coming years. [9]

Considering its strong negative impact on poverty and human development, mitigation of climate change effects has been listed at the top in the objectives of **Unified Political Theory** and the list of **Universal Common Good** identified by insightism. The principle of **Collective Responsibility of the World for Global Risks** evolved by insightism makes every country and every citizen of the world responsible for the present and future global risks, including climate change. This accountability principle is more relevant to climate change than any other global risks, because of its universal impact and accelerating threat. Further, without addressing the climate change issue, the unmanageable woes of the deprived population living in less developed nations due to unpredictable natural disasters cannot be reduced and consequently, the **Threshold Economic Justice** envisaged by insightism cannot be achieved.

The good news is that despite the rhetoric of populist against climate positive action, increasing number of people in Europe see the climate change as the greatest threat to their countries, even in this pandemic. According to a survey conducted by PEW Research Center (reported on 9th

September 2020), in 14 developed countries including European nations, the US, South Korea and Japan, majorities in all 14 countries surveyed agree that global climate change and the spread of infectious diseases pose major threats to their country. Concern about climate change is especially high in Spain, France, Italy, South Korea and Japan, with at least eight-in-ten in each country describing it as a major threat. The share of people who see global warming as a major threat is significantly higher today in nine of the 10 countries the Center has tracked over the past seven years. For instance, in the UK, 71% now say global climate change is a major threat, compared with 48% when the question was first asked in 2013 – an increase of 23 percentage points. Concern, however, has recently levelled off: In the UK and other countries tracked, worries about climate change have changed little since 2018. [10]

Insightism insists that the above fact of increasing awareness about the hazards of climate change among the people of developed nations should be spread across the world to maintain and build the momentum towards this direction and to discourage the negative propaganda of the populists. People and policy makers of developing and less developed countries should be sensitized on how the climate denialism of developed nations which are the major polluters impacts their economy and human development. With necessary supportive evidence, the leaders of less developed and developing countries which face natural disasters due to climate change, should raise this issue with the leaders of major polluting countries in every international forum directly and indirectly and force them to adhere to the agreed plans and schedules for reducing global warming. Otherwise, there should be a strong demand from all such affected countries to compensate for the losses incurred due to natural disasters from a newly created pool of funds contributed by polluting nations, applying the principle of "polluter-pays" internationally. The Paris Agreement requires each Party to prepare, communicate and maintain successive Nationally Determined Contributions (NDCs) that it intends to achieve. NDCs embody efforts by each country to reduce national emissions and adapt to the impacts of climate change. Parties shall pursue domestic mitigation measures, with the aim of achieving the objectives of such contributions towards reducing global warming. However, no sanction is proposed against the defaulter of the agreed NDCs and no monetary compensation mechanism has been created to recompense the countries which face natural disasters due to climate change effects. Hence, logically there should be a pool of funds with mandatory financial contributions from the countries which do not follow their NDCs to compensate the loses due to natural disasters. Determination of the quantum of mandatory contribution by polluting countries based on their CHGs emissions and NDCs compliance and claim of compensation towards natural disasters due to climate change effects may be a complicated task for environmental economists. However, it is high time such a compensatory mechanism is created forthwith to bring a sense of accountability among rouge polluting nations.

Right-wing populist leaders of developed nations who are already in the denial mode of climate change effects may take advantage of the sudden global economic slowdown due to COVID-19 pandemic and they may either leave the Paris Agreement as done by Donald Trump or show no interest to fulfil the committed NDCs. Such countries should be identified and exposed internationally. Activists against child labour boycott the goods involving child labour imported from developing countries. Similarly, wildlife conservation activists do not use the goods made of animal and bird hides and skins. In the same manner, the people of less developed, developing nations and developed countries which comply the NDCs to reduce global warming should boycott the goods and services exported from countries which refuse to participate in the internationally agreed climate positive actions to reach climate goals as scheduled. Involvement of youth and women and use of technology in this campaign against climate denialism will be more effective and fruitful. Without dynamic and powerful knowledge diffusion on the cataclysmic consequences of climate change across the world supported by verifiable evidences, collective consciousness of the world cannot be alerted on the current and impending challenges of climate change, and the goals of climate action cannot be reached as scheduled.

To enable to remedy the multidimensional causes (pseudo nationalism and national populism) and symptoms (polarization of society, intra-state armed conflicts, anti-poor policies and climate denialism) of behavioural disorder of state insightism strongly recommends its core ideology of dissemination of knowledge, nurturing wisdom and creation of awareness and insight on the political and socio-economic implications of such disorder within the state and globally.

9

YOUTH INSIGHTISM

Already so many teenagers from Malala Yousufzai to Greta Thunberg and Jamie Margolin to Xiye Bastida are acting at global level as the envoys of insightism diffusing knowledge, creating wisdom and providing insight on the importance of safety of biosphere, gender equality, alleviating poverty, reducing inequality etc. There are number of youth voluntary organizations working across the world towards reducing the global risks and supporting human development. According to a 2016 UNDP report, there were 1.8 billion young people between the ages of 10 and 24, which was the largest youth population the world has ever seen. This huge young population is growing up now when the world is at a critical crossroad. The present youth are smart in comprehending the complex difficulties faced by the society, resourceful and proactive in finding solutions to them and more importantly, they have the cutting edge of using the latest technology. In recent times, all around the world, they have demonstrated their ability in organizing spontaneous and peaceful uprisings using digital and communication technologies in a short period without any physical contact or charismatic leadership. They are creative, innovative and ready to face challenges in mitigating the chronic miseries of people for which they are not responsible. Participation of large number of young girls in positive activism is unprecedented in history and reassuring. With these advantages, insightism trusts that the present youth would act as its driving force in guiding the world in the path of knowledge, wisdom and insight to mitigate the global risks and achieve inclusive and sustainable human development. Insightism does not intend to teach anything new to the youth who are already into the programmes of human development and reducing global risks. It only attempts to give a new perspective to their field of activism and channelise their actions in a more optimal and sustainable way, applying the methodologies of insightism.

YOUTH ACTIVISM – CURRENT TREND

Discussing the youth activism of 2019 and 2020, Allison Reed of MOVEMENTS opines that long gone are the days in which the youth are taking a back seat to social change. One can hardly turn on the news without seeing images of mass social unrest and protests attended by people who are still too young to drive a car or cast a vote. Student and youth protests are hardly a new trend, however, with the accessibility of social media and the emerging global network of youth activism, they are better organized, more engaged, and they are calling for systemic change around the globe. 2019 saw a wave of protests across the globe, in all of which young people were an integral part and filled the streets demanding change. Many believe that this generation's social and political activism is a direct result of generational precariousness or the so-called generational desperation. This notion refers to the perceived burden felt by a generation who feels they will be paying the price for the greed, gross mismanagement, and irresponsibility of the previous generation of political and economic elites. Today's youth activists and protestors rely heavily on social media and technology to engage their peers. By capitalizing on and mastering technology to connect with others, a shift has taken place within youth activism with the rise of so-called "Alter-Activism." Alter-Activism emphasizes shared living experiences and connectivity amongst young activists. Young protesters continue to distance themselves from formal political parties and established party line ideologies. They invest more time and attention in novel technologies, new forms of thought, valuable deliberation, open dialogue, and consensus-building within movements. Youth Alter-Activism stands as a direct counterpoint to multi-party politics, religious sectarianism, and dogmatic debates over representative democracy. Perhaps the most important characteristic of the new wave of youth protests is that they are leaderless. Using social media as a key tool for creating awareness, mobilizing, and organizing movements, youth protests can capitalize on spontaneity to keep energy behind their campaigns instead of relying on charismatic leaders. Maintaining leaderless movements is particularly important to those movements happening in repressive countries, where the movement can continue even as governments arrest protestors and shutter challenges of communication. Youth political engagement and social movements of the last year focus on a variety of issues, from socio-economic grievances, climate change and environmental protections, political freedoms, gender equality, LGBTQ+ rights, and clearly shows that this generation is a force for change. While these systemic and pervasive issues uniquely affect the global youth, they show a willingness to work with others to recognize the interconnectivity of the world around them and demand change. [1]

The current trend of activism of the youth as described above is perfectly in sync with the ideologically neutral global approach of insightism towards politics, religion, form of government and regional, social, racial and gender differences. Similarly, the global reach of youth activism is also in tune with the **'Unified Political Theory'**, **'Collective Responsibility for Global Risks'**, **'Universal Common Good'**, **'Threshold Economic Justice'** and other global concepts of insightism.

EMERGENCE OF YOUNG LEADERS

Aryn Baker of TIME magazine says that a new generation of leaders inspired by activist movements is driving change around the world. She narrates that over the past year, citizens in Africa, Asia, Europe, Latin America and the Middle East took to the streets to raise their voices against inequality, corruption and bad governance. And while from Italy to Iraq and Venezuela to Zimbabwe they promoted wildly differing slogans, the subtext was always the same: the system is not working. The youth at the forefront of these movements are no longer content to just push for change from the fringes of power. Increasingly they are taking the reins themselves, either through the democratic process or by spearheading protest movements that command the world's attention.

Countries such as France, Ireland, Austria and Ukraine are turning to younger leaders and new styles of leadership. In December 2019 Finland's Sanna Marin, 34, became the world's youngest Prime Minister, only to be upstaged a few weeks later by the return of Austria's Sebastian Kurz, who was sworn in as Chancellor for a second term at the age of 33 on January 2020. Kurz and Marin are the latest in a wave of politicians in their 30s winning leadership roles, including New Zealand's Prime Minister Jacinda Ardern (39), Ukraine's Prime Minister Oleksiy Honcharuk (35) and El Salvador's President Nayib Bukele (38).

Society is no longer passing the baton to the next in line in a continuing trend of incremental change. We are witnessing a fundamental departure from politics as usual, as these young leaders respond to the demands of even younger activists acutely attuned to the injustices and inequalities of their era. What unites these movements is a desire to tear down and rebuild structures built by past generations. In Europe, the experience of post-recession austerity measures has cemented a new commitment to social reforms and greater public spending among the young, and their leaders are following suit. Youth-led protests in Hong Kong, India and Sudan are rebelling against conservative and repressive leadership, while in Iraq and Chile they are demanding an end to corruption. In Lebanon, where anti-government protests drew a quarter of the population to the streets, young protesters have called for a complete overhaul of what they see as a broken political system. Across the Middle East, the outsize hopes engendered by the 2010 Arab Spring uprisings have been shattered by harsh government crackdowns combined with economic stagnation, according to a new survey of Arab youth.

The experience of today's older generations might suggest that the young will shift rightward as their stakes in society grow. After all, today's conservative-voting boomers came of age amid the countercultural revolutions of the 1960s. But today's youth are unlikely to shed their progressive values over time, according to current research. "Young people now are more socially liberal than young people were in the past," says Matt Henn, a professor of social research at the U.K.'s Nottingham Trent University. "People's views on key values such as concerns over the climate emergency, support for investment in public services rather than privatization … are not necessarily going to dissipate over time. These are fundamental values that, research suggests, broadly stay with people into later life." [2]

Insightism subscribes fully to the above view that young and efficient leaders are going to rule many countries in future and like the leaders of their previous generations, they will not compromise with their ideologies deviating from their progressive and liberal approach at any point of their political career, as the emerging political philosophy will take a new path towards prioritizing the basic needs for the sustenance of global community and protection of the biosphere, giving importance to universal common good, overriding all other national and global issues.

YOUTH INSIGHTISM

Current youth activist movements and activists are already following the methodologies of insightism in the process of reversing the trend of global warming and reducing inequalities, poverty and armed conflicts by educating the public and creating necessary awareness on the calamitous consequences of above global risks. However, in the present global political situation, where full democracy is not practiced in majority of the countries and national populism is on the rise everywhere, the words 'activism' and 'activist' are increasingly interpreted with negative connotations. Even a logical, factual and constructive kind of dissenting remark of an activist about the functioning of government within a country, make the activist "anti-national" attracting sedition law. If the activist happens to be an outsider, his action is termed as "foreign ploy to destabilise the country". To avoid this kind of insinuating allegations and declare apparently that all the youth activists are ambassadors of knowledge and their primary objective is only to give insight and create awareness about the persistent social, economic and environmental ailments, the present trend of 'alter-activism' of the youth may be termed more appropriately as **'Youth Insightism'**. This simple change in terminology will tend to give a positive universal outlook and narrative about the voluntary activities of young people with the only objective of improving the living conditions of the people by creating necessary awareness and absolutely with no intention of disrupting the government functioning.

The youth insightists may propagate the ideologies of insightism exclusively or along with their area of activism, which will add value to the scope of such activism. To enable to divert the attention of the public and political leaders from the rhetoric of the current political philosophies which have become unsuitable to address the global risks, all youth insightists irrespective of their sphere of activity may popularize the **Unified Political Theory** of insightism with its following initial objectives:

1. Safeguarding the biosphere from the catastrophic damages of climate change.

2. Providing basic conditions required for everyone in the world to acquire one's capability by adulthood that enables one to function independently in society.

3. Maintaining a peaceful, harmonious and sustainable world order.

Youth insightists may explain the importance of the following **Universal Common Good** identified by insightism to enable to achieve the above objectives of the Unified Political Theory.

i. Taking climate positive action as planned and agreed internationally.

ii. Complete eradication of extreme poverty in all forms, everywhere.

iii. Controlling fast-growing economic inequality within and between countries before reaching the breaking point.

iv. Moderating and eliminating the causes of large-scale and religious armed conflicts and international terrorism.

To deliver the above universal common good, the following concepts of insightism need to be propagated widely, so that all governments and their citizens can understand and incorporate them in their government/political agenda and demands:

i. Collective Responsibility for Global Risks

ii. Right to become a person

iii. Self Potentialisation

iv. Threshold Economic Justice

v. Women Development is Sustainable Development

vi. Rationalization and Irradicalization

As a kind of disclaimer to all governments, the entire spectrum of youth insightists of all countries shall make it amply clear to the world that any peaceful and lawful method followed by them towards attaining the above universal common good directly or indirectly in a country or outside the country is to be construed as in the process of protecting the right to life of all human beings of the world, as millions of lives are lost every year due to the perilous effect of major global risks. Since the 'right to life of a person' is an absolute right that cannot be interfered by any state, the peaceful and lawful activities of youth to protect this right by reducing global risks cannot be interpreted as "anti-national" or "foreign ploy to destabilise a country" by any government. Even after this, if a government takes action against the youth insightists involved in lawful activities towards achieving the universal common good, such a government should be exposed internationally revealing its lack of concern for universal common good and respect for right to life of all human beings and there should be a strong campaign to isolate such government internationally with appropriate sanctions till it changes its views. Parallelly, a strong public opinion should be built across the world for the governments to listen to the voices of the youth without disregarding them, interact with them in a meaningful manner, understand and appreciate their apprehensions, and attempt to comply to their reasonable demands nationally and internationally, as far as possible. Snubbing and condemning the spirited expressions of the budding, unselfish, purposeful and socially responsible youth to build a better world would tantamount to gross mismanagement of our valuable human resources that are the only hope for our future.

Technology – Cutting Edge for Youth

The youth are already using the latest digital technology in alter-activism to organize movements instantly and communicate their messages and ideas to general public with the aim to improve their quality of life. Contrarily, populists, radicals and extremists use the digital platforms and technology extensively to disseminate their exclusive narratives in order to pursue their respective ideologies and vested interests. These kinds of attractive narratives misdirect the attention of the public from the real and critical issues of the society leading to its polarization, generate violence and conflicts by radicalizing youth to take up arms for pseudo national causes and by grooming extremism keep the world under the constant threat of terrorism. Rising right-wing populists' propagation of anti-poor policies against globalization, immigration, minorities and climate positive action block the efforts to mitigate the global risks which tend to add the sufferings of poor. Identifying and grouping people on the pseudo nationalistic issues of religion, religious sectarian divisions and ethnic identity within the country make such countries fragile and conflict affected, where the world population living in extreme poor conditions is getting converged. Radicalization based on religious fundamentalism pose security threat across the world. All the above forces use high-end digital information and communication technology, digital social and private platforms, and even hire business analytics firms for their campaigns and execution of their plans. Though they function with different objectives, one common factor among all these elements is that they disseminate lies, half-truths and post-truths, superimposing facts and ideologies, orchestrating history and hiding/exaggerating the current events and their backgrounds, without any concern for their national interest and social cohesion or the common interest of the global community. Since these are recently emerging problems with complicated dimensions, supported with modern technology, there are no global plans to address them effectively, either with the UN or any other international agencies. This kind of projection of emotional illusions can be comprehended and their disrupting negative effects can be nullified only by the youth with their latest technological and analytical skills. The sensory distortion of the public due to exposure to the above emotional illusions can be corrected by the process of rationalization and irradicalization discussed in the previous chapter. With their exceptional skill and ability to use internet, social media, apps and information and communication technology, youth can only engineer the above processes of rationalization and irradicalization successfully to sensitize and enlighten the public.

According to Renata Dessallien, UN Resident Coordinator in India just as electricity allowed us to tame time, enabling us to radically alter almost every aspect of existence, Artificial Intelligence (AI) can leapfrog us toward eradicating hunger, poverty and disease — opening up new and hitherto unimaginable pathways for climate change mitigation, education and scientific discovery. A study published in *Nature* reviewing the impact of AI on the Sustainable Development Goals (SDGs) finds that AI may act as an enabler on 134 — or 79% — of all SDG targets and it can actively hinder 59 — or 35% — of SDG targets. [3] Like in any other walk of life, if optimally utilized, technology is going to play a big and crucial role in addressing the global risks and ensuring the sustainable human development, as stated above. Youth alone can handle this modern technology now and in near future. If the present youth having cutting edge in technology are attuned towards the urgency and importance of addressing the global risks and accomplishing the SDGs as scheduled, they can bring a miraculous and less disruptive revolution using their skills and contemporary technology to suddenly change the world a better place to live in for the present and future generations.

Non-Consumption Movement

Everyone knows that the entire world and all domains of human activities are becoming increasingly commercial, slowly debunking the age-old personal, family and social value systems. The realpolitik has replaced traditional politics. With quantum growth in wealth and influential network, the exponentially rising corporate sector is gradually acquiring itself a commanding position in all parts of world, enabling it to dictate terms to the political and economic decisions of all sorts of governments. The nexus between the business sector and the government and political leaders across the spectrum of political ideologies is growing strongly. But whatever be the power of the MNCs, they ultimately have to depend on the market and general public who consume their goods and services for their survival and growth. Any dent in the market for particular goods or services is going to hurt the corporate entities which supply such goods and services which in turn would impact the economic interest of the country in which such businesses are located. Therefore, in this globally commercialised era, the best and simple way to sensitize a country/ MNC which acts against global common good would be to identify the products/services supplied from such country/MNC globally and begin an international movement against the consumption of such identified goods and services, till the country/MNC corrects its course. Similar non-violent movements like 'Non-cooperation Movement' and 'Swadeshi Movement' (consumption of indigenously produced goods only) of Gandhiji were very successful during India's independent struggle. In today's digital world, it is easier to run such non-consumption movement supported with convincing reasons and clear objectives. Youth insightists may use the methodology of **'Non-Consumption Movement'** whenever required to sensitize the public and governments on specific important issues concerning global risks, and to focus the attention of the world on such issues and pressurize the countries/MNCs responsible for the problems to address them.

Simple Guidelines

All youth insightists will be committed to the following simple guidelines of insightism in order to achieve success in their goals, avoiding unnecessary intervention and harassment by the state.

1. The major mission of youth insightism shall be dissemination of necessary knowledge, creating wisdom and providing insight on the major global risks among the public concerned, that will enable them to identify appropriate solution to the problems, objectively.

2. All youth insightists shall understand that curing the present congenital and behavioural disorders of state is the only way to address the global risks and mitigate them permanently by applying the methodologies of insightism directly or indirectly towards this goal.

3. All youth insightists shall acquire necessary skills in technology for the above purposes and such skills shall not be misused.

4. While generating funds for their campaigns, they shall be extra careful in avoiding contributions from different vested interest groups.

5. All their activities shall follow non-violent and non-disruptive means.

6. Their movements shall be completely apolitical.

7. There shall not be any kind of association with commercial activities or organizations.

8. They shall be neutral to all kinds of strata or divisions that exist in community/society.

9. No negative remarks shall be made against any past or current political, economic and social ideologies and the persons associated with such ideologies.

10. Only objective comments shall be made explaining what is going wrong now in their field of insightism, how it affects the life of people and what are the remedial measures to be taken towards achieving what kind of positive output.

11. There shall be a persistent effort to inter-connect the world for constructive purposes towards bonding the global community, so that all kinds of perceptual differences prevailing in different societies can disappear naturally.

12. Youth insightists shall always start their campaign initially among their peer groups, family members and local community to get their initial approval. This approval will encourage them to expand their activities further.

13. All young persons need not be transformed into insightists. Willingly volunteering youth alone may act as insightists. Making them aware of the objectives of insightism will be sufficient.

14. All activities of youth insightism shall be made transparent through web portals or blogs and all their financial transactions shall be made public in a periodical manner.

15. Youth insightists may enter in to politics. However, after such transformation, he/she shall cease to be an insightist.

WORDS OF CAUTION

World is already in the flux of retrogressive political conditions and catastrophic global risks. This entropic situation is getting further complicated with the prolonging pandemic. For the present youth, the future appears to be challenging and more particularly for the majority of the young population living in less developed and developing countries, the forthcoming days are going to be harsher. Insightism has identified the root cause of the present problems that hamper the progress in addressing the global risks and connected human development issues and suggested a few simple and implementable solutions to resolve them. These findings and recommendations may not be exactly correct and comprehensive. An attempt has been made to introduce a new political perspective, considering the historical and current political and global problems while deviating from the conventional western political philosophy, so that it will generate healthy debates and discussions mainly among youth that may lead to deeper understanding of the issues and more precise solutions to the problems. One thing that insightism firmly believes is that without the active involvement of the present youth and the empowerment of women, the global risks can never be addressed successfully and resolved permanently and we cannot reach the goals of sustainable human development as planned. Everyone should understand that the future of mankind and all living organisms of our biosphere is in the hands of the youth and women of the present generation. It is the collective responsibility of all to think and act accordingly. If we succeed in this endeavour, it would be a crowning achievement of human civilization.

ANNEXURE – I

Probable List of 50 Countries Currently Suffering from Congenital Disorder Due to Lack of Political Legitimacy

(From worst to bad)

FSI Ranking	Fragile State Index (FSI) – Bottom 50 countries	Human Development Index 2020 Ranking	Economic Freedom Index 2020 Ranking	Corruption Perception Index 2020 Ranking
1	Yemen	11	Not ranked	4
2	Somalia	Not ranked	Not ranked	1
3	South Sudan	4	Not ranked	1
4	Syria	38	Not ranked	3
5	Congo (Democratic Republic)	15	19	9
6	Central African Republic	2	22	33
7	Chad	3	20	17
8	Sudan	19	8	6
9	Afghanistan	21	45	12

FSI Ranking	Fragile State Index (FSI) – Bottom 50 countries	Human Development Index 2020 Ranking	Economic Freedom Index 2020 Ranking	Corruption Perception Index 2020 Ranking
10	Zimbabwe	40	7	23
11	Cameroon	37	36	25
12	Burundi	5	15	12
13	Haiti	20	28	9
14	Nigeria	29	Above 50	25
15	Guinea	12	Above 50	40
16	Mali	6	Above 50	48
17	Iraq	Above 50	Not ranked	17
18	Eritrea	10	4	17
19	Niger	1	44	Above 50
20	Libya	Above 50	Not ranked	8
21	Ethiopia	17	35	Above 50
22	Myanmar	43	40	40
23	Guinea Bissau	14	33	12
24	Uganda	31	Above 50	36
25	Pakistan	36	46	49
26	Congo (Republic)	41	5	12
27	Mozambique	9	21	25
28	Venezuela	Above 50	2	4

29	Kenya	47	49	49
30	North Korea	Not ranked	1	9
31	Liberia	13	16	40
32	Cote d'Ivoire	28	Above 50	Above 50
33	Mauritania	33	Above 50	45
34	Angola	42	27	36
35	Rwanda	30	Above 50	Above 50
36	Egypt	Above 50	39	Above 50
37	Burkina Faso	8	Above 50	Above 50
38	Togo	23	41	45
39	Bangladesh	Above 50	Above 50	33
40	Lebanon	Above 50	24	25
41	Zambia	44	34	Above 50
42	Sierra Leone	7	13	Above 50
43	Malawi	16	29	48
44	Iran	Above 50	17	25
45	Eswatini	Above 50	50	Above 50
46	Equatorial Guinea	45	14	6
47	Djibouti	24	30	36
48	Timor-Leste	49	10	Above 50
49	Nepal	48	42	Above 50
50	Papua New Guinea	35	Above 50	36

Source

1. Fund For Peace, FRAGILE STATES INDEX, ANNUAL REPORT 2020

   https://fundforpeace.org/wp-content/uploads/2020/05/fsi2020-report.pdf

2. UNDP, Human Development Reports, HDR 2020

   http://hdr.undp.org/sites/default/files/hdr2020.pdf

3. The Heritage Foundation, 2020 Index of Economic Freedom

   https://www.heritage.org/index/

4. Transparency International, Corruption Perceptions Index, 2020

   https://www.transparency.org/en/cpi/2020/index/nzl

ANNEXURE – II

FY20 List of Fragile and Conflict-affected Situations
(Suffering from Congenital Disorder of State)

High-Intensity Conflict	High Institutional and Social Fragility
1. Afghanistan	**Non-small States**
2. Central African Republic	1. Chad
3. Libya	2. Congo, Rep.
4. Somalia	3. Eritrea
5. South Sudan	4. Gambia, The
6. Syrian Arab Rep.	5. Guinea-Bissau
7. Yemen, Rep.	6. Haiti
Medium-Intensity Conflict	7. Kosovo
1. Burkina Faso	8. Lebanon
2. Burundi	9. Liberia
3. Cameroon	10. Myanmar
4. Congo, Dem. Rep.	11. Papua New Guinea
5. Iraq	12. Venezuela, RB

Medium-Intensity Conflict	High Institutional and Social Fragility - Non-small States
6. Mali	13. Zimbabwe
7. Niger	14. West Bank and Gaza (territory)
8. Nigeria	
9. Sudan	
	Small Sates
	1. Comoros
	2. Kiribati
	3. Marshall Islands
	4. Micronesia, Fed. Sts.
	5. Solomon Islands
	6. Timor-Leste
	7. Tuvalu

Source: The World Bank, IBRD-IDA, Classification of Fragile and Conflict-Affected Situations
https://www.worldbank.org/en/topic/fragilityconflictviolence/brief/harmonized-list-of- fragile-situations

ANNEXURE – III

List of Countries Ruled by Right-wing Populist Governments Suffering from Behavioural Disorder of State due to Neo-Nationalism

Country	Leader	Party
Australia	Scott Morrison	Liberal–National Coalition
Austria	Norbert Hofer	Freiheitliche Partei Österreichs
Brazil	Jair Bolsonaro	Alliance for Brazil
Bulgaria	Veselin Mareshki	Volya
Estonia	Mart Helme	Eesti Konservatiivne Rahvaerakond
Hungary	Viktor Orbán	Fidesz
India	Narendra Modi	Bharatiya Janata Party
Israel	Benjamin Netanyahu	Likud
Japan	Shinzō Abe	Jiyū-Minshutō
Latvia	Artuss Kaimiņš	Kam pieder valsts?
Montenegro	Andrija Mandić (and others)	Demokratski front

Country	Leader	Party
Netherlands	Geert Wilders	Partij voor de Vrijheid
Norway	Siv Jensen	Framstegspartiet
Philippines	Rodrigo Duterte	Hugpong
Pakistan	Imran Khan	Pakistan Tehrik-e-Insaaf
Poland	Jarosław Kaczyński	Prawo i Sprawiedliwość
Serbia	Nenad Popović	Serbian People's Party
Slovenia	Janez Jansa	Slovenska demokratska stranka
Switzerland	Albert Rösti	Swiss People's Party
Thailand	Prayut Chan-o-cha	Palang Pracharat
Turkey	Recep Tayyip Erdogan	Adalet ve Kalkinma Partisi
UK	Boris Johnson	Conservative Party; UKIP
USA	Donald Trump (till Jan 2021)	Republican Party (till Jan 2021)

Source: Annalisa Merelli, QUARTZ, The state of global right-wing populism in 2019, Dec 30, 2019

https://qz.com/1774201/the-global-state-of-right-wing-populism-in-2019/

REFERENCES

1. INTRODUCTION

1. United Nations, Global Issues, Climate Change

   https://www.un.org/en/sections/issues-depth/climate-change/

2. NASA Global Climate Change, The effects of Climate Change,

   https://climate.nasa.gov/effects/

3. GSDRC, Climate Change and social development, Topic Guide, July 2016, page-1

   https://gsdrc.org/wp-content/uploads/2016/07/GSDRC_CC_SocDev.pdf

4. UNHCR, Global Trends: Forced Displacement in 2019

   https://www.unhcr.org/5ee200e37.pdf

5. The World Counts, Oct 2020,

   https://www.theworldcounts.com/challenges/people-and-poverty/hunger-and-obesity/how-many-people-die-from-hunger-each-year/story

6. The World Bank Group, Poverty, Overview, Oct 07, 2020

   https://www.worldbank.org/en/topic/poverty/overview

7. Eric Jensen, Teaching with Poverty in Mind, Chap-1

   http://www.ascd.org/publications/books/109074/chapters/Understanding-the-Nature-of-Poverty.aspx

8. Piketty, Thomas (2014). Capital in the Twenty-First Century. Belknap Press. ISBN 067443000X p. 571

9. GSDRC, Inequality and Human Development, Human Development Rreport 2005, Summary

   https://gsdrc.org/document-library/inequality-and-human-development/#:~:text=Inequality%20is%20a%20fundamental%20issue,and%20different%20regions%20and%20groups

10. Human Development Report 2019, Overview

    http://hdr.undp.org/sites/default/files/hdr_2019_overview_-_english.pdf

11. Remarks of Bill Gates, Harvard Commencement 2007 on 7/6/2007

12. UN, A New Era of Conflict and Violence,

    https://www.un.org/en/un75/new-era-conflict-and-violence

13. Frances Stewart, Root causes of violent conflict in developing countries, Journal List BMJ v.324(7333); 2002 Feb 9 PMC1122271

    https://www.ncbi.nlm.nih.gov/pmc/articles/PMC1122271/

14. Olivia Giovetti, Concern Worldwide US, Forced Migration: 6 Causes and Examples, June 28, 2019

    https://www.concernusa.org/story/forced-migration-causes/

15. UNHCR, Global Trends: Forced Displacement in 2019

    https://www.unhcr.org/5ee200e37.pdf

16. UN, Department of Economic and Social Affairs, Sustainable Development, Transforming our world: the 2030 Agenda for Sustainable Development, Preamble

    https://sdgs.un.org/2030agenda

17. Hannah Ritchie and Max Roser, Sep 20, 2018, Our World in Data, Now it is possible to take stock – did the world achieve the Millennium Development Goals?

    https://ourworldindata.org/millennium-development-goals

18. © Bertelsmann Stiftung and Sustainable Development Solutions Network, June 2019, Sustainable Development Report 2019, Executive Summary

    https://s3.amazonaws.com/sustainabledevelopment.report/2019/2019_sustainable_development_report.pdf

2. CONGENITAL AND BEHAVIOURAL DISORDERS OF MODERN STATE

1. Kissinger, Henry (2014). World Order. ISBN 978-0-698-16572-4 – page-26

2. Legitimacy (political). In *Wikipedia, The Free Encyclopedia*, February 7, 2021

    https://en.wikipedia.org/w/index.php?title=Legitimacy_(political)&oldid=991857442

3. Pierre Manent, An Intellectual History of Liberalism (1994) pp. 20–38

4. Henry Kissinger, World Order – Reflections on the Character of Nations and the Course of History – Allan Lane an imprint of Penguin Books – p-3

5. Henry Kissinger, World Order – Reflections on the Character of Nations and the Course of History – Allan Lane an imprint of Penguin Books – p-363

6. Motyl, Alexander J. (2001). Encyclopedia of Nationalism, Volume II. Academic Press. ISBN 0-12-227230-7

7. National Identity and Mental Illness: The Double Helix of Modern Politics

    https://ecpr.eu/Filestore/paperproposal/cb3f003e-04ed-42c0-a597-d126fda90d3c.pdf

3. MAJOR SUFFERINGS OF DISORDERS

1. History.com Editors, French Revolution, Nov 9, 2009/Feb 4, 2021

    https://www.history.com/topics/france/french-revolution

2. The Editors of Encyclopaedia Britannica, Nation-state, Politics, Mar 23, 2020

   https://www.britannica.com/topic/nation-state

3. Andreas Wimmer. Waves of War: Nationalism, State Formation, and Ethnic Exclusion in the Modern World. Cambridge Studies in Comparative Politics Series. Cambridge: Cambridge University Press, 2013

4. Rand Corporation, Lasting Consequences of World War II Means More Illness, Lower Education and Fewer Chances to Marry for Survivors, Jan 21, 2014

   https://www.rand.org/news/press/2014/01/21/index1.html

5. History.com Editors, Nazi Party, Nov 9, 2009/Mar 30, 2020

   https://www.history.com/topics/world-war-ii/nazi-party

6. BBC NEWS, Balkans war: a brief guide, 18 Mar, 2016

   https://www.bbc.com/news/world-europe-17632399

7. COUNCIL on FOREIGN RELATIONS, Excerpt: The World and Yugoslavia's Wars, Book by Richard H. Ullman,

   https://www.cfr.org/excerpt-world-and-yugoslavias-wars

8. Wikipedia, The Free Encyclopedia, Rwandan genocide, Page Version ID: 1005171215, 6 Feb, 2021/11 Feb, 2021

   https://en.wikipedia.org/w/index.php?title=Rwandan_genocide&oldid=1005171215

9. ROBERT I. ROTBERG, Failed States, Collapsed States, Weak States: Causes and Indicators, p-1

   https://www.brookings.edu/wp-content/uploads/2016/07/statefailureandstateweaknessinatimeofterror_chapter.pdf

10. Prof. Clionadh Raleigh, ACLED, Forward to TEN CONFLICTS TO WORRYABOUT IN 2020, Jan 2020

    https://acleddata.com/acleddatanew/wp-content/uploads/2020/01/ACLED_TenConflicts2020_FinalWeb.pdf

11. Matthias Basedau, GIGA, The Rise of Religious Armed Conflicts in Sub-Saharan Africa: No Simple Answers, Number: 4 | 08/2017 | ISSN: 1862-3603

    https://www.giga-hamburg.de/en/publications/11576059-rise-religious-armed-conflicts-saharan-africa-simple-answers/

12. Bettina Koch, E-International Relations, Unmasking 'Religious' Conflicts and Religious Radicalisation in the Middle East, 17 May, 2019

    https://www.e-ir.info/2019/05/17/unmasking-religious-conflicts-and-religious-radicalisation-in-the-middle-east/

13. BBC News, Why is there a war in Syria? Feb 25, 2019

    https://www.bbc.com/news/world-middle-east-35806229

14. Amnesty International, Syria 2019

    https://www.amnesty.org/en/countries/middle-east-and-north-africa/syria/report-syria/

4. COMPREHENSIVE AND ENFORCEABLE STATE LEGITIMACY

1. CLAIRE MCLOUGHLIN, DLP, State Legitimacy, Dec 2014

    https://www.dlprog.org/publications/research-papers/state-legitimacy

2. GSDRC, State Legitimacy, Topic Guide, Apr 2016

    https://gsdrc.org/topic-guides/state-society-relations-and-citizenship/state-legitimacy/

3. GSRDC, Fragile States, Topic Guide, Mar 2016

    https://gsdrc.org/wp-content/uploads/2016/03/FragileStates.pdf

4. Schultze-Kraft, M., and Rew, M. (2014) How Does State Fragility Affect Rural Development?, GIZ, Germany

    https://opendocs.ids.ac.uk/opendocs/handle/20.500.12413/3950

5. Nancy Lindborg, Handle with care:The challenge of fragility

    https://www.brookings.edu/wp-content/uploads/2017/08/global-20170731-blum-nancylindborg-brief-4.pdf

6. Norad Report 20/2009 Discussion, The Legitimacy of the State in Fragile Situations, Feb 2009

    http://www.institut-gouvernance.org/docs/the_legitimacy_of_the_state_in_fragile_situations.pdf

7. Aoife McCullough, GSDRC, The legitimacy of states and armed non-state actors, Topic Guide, July 2015

    https://gsdrc.org/topic-guides/the-legitimacy-of-states-and-armed-non-state-actors/key-language-and-concepts/approaches-to-assessing-legitimacy-2/

8. Fund For Peace, FRAGILE STATES INDEX, ANNUAL REPORT 2020

    https://fundforpeace.org/wp-content/uploads/2020/05/fsi2020-report.pdf

9. UNDP, Human Development Reports, HDR 2020

    http://hdr.undp.org/sites/default/files/hdr2020.pdf

10. The World Bank, IBRD-IDA, Classification of Fragile and Conflict-Affected Situations

    https://www.worldbank.org/en/topic/fragilityconflictviolence/brief/harmonized-list-of-fragile-situations

11. The Heritage Foundation, 2020 Index of Economic Freedom

    https://www.heritage.org/index/

12. Transparency International, Corruption Perceptions Index, 2020

    https://www.transparency.org/en/cpi/2020/index/nzl

13. GSRDC, Fragile States, Topic Guide, Mar 2016

    https://gsdrc.org/wp-content/uploads/2016/03/FragileStates.pdf

14. Nancy Lindborg, Handle with care:The challenge of fragility

https://www.brookings.edu/wp-content/uploads/2017/08/global-20170731-blum-nancylindborg-brief-4.pdf

5. NATIONALISM TO RIGHT-WING POPULISM

1. Hans Kohn, Britannica, Nationalism – Politics

https://www.britannica.com/topic/nationalism

2. Ezaz Ahmed, Observer Research Foundation, Understanding the different shades of populism around the world, Aug 14, 2019

https://www.orfonline.org/expert-speak/understanding-the-different-shades-of-populism-around-the-world-54429/

3. Annalisa Merelli, QUARTZ, The state of global right-wing populism in 2019, Dec 30, 2019

https://qz.com/1774201/the-global-state-of-right-wing-populism-in-2019/

4. Matthew Lockwood, Oxford Research Group, Right-Wing Populism and Climate Change Policy, 13 June, 2019

https://www.oxfordresearchgroup.org.uk/blog/right-wing-populism-and-climate-change-policy

5. Grace Waldee, The Effects of Nationalism and Populism on Political Participation

https://www.ucis.pitt.edu/esc/system/files/resources/images/EDC-Grace-Waldee_0.pdf

6. G. John Ikenberry, OXFORD Academic, International Affairs, The end of liberal international order? Jan 01, 2018

https://academic.oup.com/ia/article/94/1/7/4762691

7. Lisa Wade, PhD, Sociological Images, Why is nationalism dangerous? July 25, 2016

https://socimages.tumblr.com/post/147951994050/why-is-nationalism-dangerous-by-lisa-wade-phd-in

8. Federico Finchelstein, Federico (2019) From Fascism to Populism in History Berkeley, California: University of California Press. pp.5-6 ISBN 9780520309357

6. INSIGHTISM

1. Richard J. Arneson, Britannica, Political Philosophy, Contemporary Questions, 29 Oct, 2020

    https://www.britannica.com/topic/political-philosophy/Foucault-and-postmodernism#ref283706

2. Political Philosophy, Wikipedia, Wikimedia Foundation, 09 Nov, 2020/12 Nov, 2020

    https://en.wikipedia.org/wiki/Political_philosophy#:~:text=Political%20philosophy%2C%20also%20known%20as,what%20form%20it%20should%20take%2C

3. Miller, David, Political Philosophy, Article Summary, Routledge Encyclopedia of Philosophy, DOI 10.4324/9780415249126-S099-1

    https://www.rep.routledge.com/articles/overview/political-philosophy/v-1

4. The Economist, Intelligence Unit, Democracy Index 2020

    https://www.eiu.com/n/campaigns/democracy-index-2020/#:~:text=Democracy%20was%20dealt%20a%20major,lives%20from%20a%20novel%20coronavirus.

5. Richard J. Arneson, Britannica, Political Philosophy, Contemporary Questions, 29 Oct, 2020

    https://www.britannica.com/topic/political-philosophy/Foucault-and-postmodernism#ref283706

6. George Eaton, Francis Fukuyama interview: "Socialism ought to come back", NewStatesman, 17 Oct, 2018

    https://www.newstatesman.com/culture/observations/2018/10/francis-fukuyama-interview-socialism-ought-come-back

7. Royale Scuderi, What Are the Differences Between Knowledge, Wisdom, and Insight?

    https://www.lifehack.org/articles/communication/what-are-the-differences-between-knowledge-wisdom-and-insight.html

8. The Economic Times, 09 Jan, 2018

    https://economictimes.indiatimes.com/news/science/ignorance-causes-problems-like-racism-bigotry-fanaticism-lead-correcting-intro/articleshow/62431435.cms?from=mdr

9. Mischa Hildebrand, Democracy Is Failing, Why Our Political System Doesn't Work in the 21st Century, May 25, 2019

    https://medium.com/@PhiJay/democracy-is-failing-2ad03247ca99

10. Elinor Burkett, Britannica, Feminism, 23 Sep, 2020

    https://www.britannica.com/topic/feminism

11. Laura D'Andrea Tyson & Jeni Klugman, Women's economic empowerment is the smart thing to do. What's stopping us? World Economic Forum, 17 Jan, 2017

    https://www.weforum.org/agenda/2017/01/womens-economic-empowerment-is-the-smart-and-right-thing-to-do-whats-stopping-us/#:~:text=The%20human%20development%2C%20economic%20and,growth%2C%20and%20greater%20international%20competitiveness

7. THERAPY FOR CONGENITAL DISORDER OF STATE

1. Adriana Conconi & Mariana Viollaz, OpenMind BBVA, Poverty, Inequality and Development: a Discussion from the Capability Approach's Framework,

    https://www.bbvaopenmind.com/en/articles/poverty-inequality-and-development-a-discussion-from-the-capability-approach-s-framework/

2. CNBCAFRICA, Why money alone can't help beat poverty in Africa, here's what is needed, 17 Aug, 2018

    https://www.cnbcafrica.com/2018/why-money-alone-cant-help-beat-poverty-in-africa-heres-what-is-needed/

3. Thomas Piketty, The Belknap Press of Harvard University Press, Capital in the Twenty First Century, pp-20, 21

4. The World Bank, IBRD-IDA, Fragility, Conflict & Violence, 01 Oct, 2020

    https://www.worldbank.org/en/topic/fragilityconflictviolence/overview

5. Robert Muggah & Ali Velshi, World Economic Forum, Religious violence is on the rise. What can faith-based communities do about it? 25 Feb, 2019

    https://www.weforum.org/agenda/2019/02/how-should-faith-communities-halt-the-rise-in-religious-violence/

8. REMEDY FOR BEHAVIOURAL DISORDER OF STATE

1. Rana Dasgupta, The Guardian, The demise of the nation state, 5 Apr, 2018

    https://www.theguardian.com/news/2018/apr/05/demise-of-the-nation-state-rana-dasgupta

2. Florian Bieber, Taylor & Francis Online, Is Nationalism on the Rise? Assessing Global Trends, 24 Oct, 2018

    https://www.tandfonline.com/doi/full/10.1080/17449057.2018.1532633

3. PIIE, What Is Globalization? And How Has the Global Economy Shaped the United States?

    https://www.piie.com/microsites/globalization/what-is-globalization#:~:text=Globalization%20is%20the%20word%20used,investment%2C%20people%2C%20and%20information.

4. Pranab Bardhan, Ideas For India, Deconstructing the global wave of right-wing populism, 08 Feb, 2017

    https://www.ideasforindia.in/topics/governance/deconstructing-the-global-wave-of-right-wing-populism.html

5. Angel Gurría, OECD, Challenges and Solutions for Globalisation, 12 Sep, 2017

    https://www.oecd.org/about/secretary-general/challenges-and-solutions-for-globalisation.htm

6. The World Bank, Moving for Prosperity: Global Migration and Labor Markets,

    https://www.worldbank.org/en/research/publication/moving-for-prosperity

7. Colonization, Wikipedia, The Free Encyclopedia, 30 Mar, 2021/04 Apr, 2021

    https://en.wikipedia.org/w/index.php?title=Colonization&oldid=1015033839

8. Richard Calland, QRIUS, Countering climate denialism requires taking on right-wing populism, 12 Feb, 2020

    https://qrius.com/countering-climate-denialism-requires-taking-on-right-wing-populism/

9. Robert Huber, Interview #38 — Populism and Climate Change, Mar 25, 2020

    https://populismobserver.com/2020/03/25/interview-38-populism-and-climate-change/

10. Pew Research Center, Despite Pandemic, Many Europeans Still See Climate Change as Greatest Threat to Their Countries, 09 Sep, 2020

    https://www.pewresearch.org/global/2020/09/09/despite-pandemic-many-europeans-still-see-climate-change-as-greatest-threat-to-their-countries/

9. YOUTH INSIGHTISM

1. Allison Reed, Movements, Global Youth Activism, Aug 11, 2020

    https://www.movements.org/en/blog/GlobalYouthActivism/

2. TIME, Aryn Baker, A New Generation of Leaders Inspired By Activist Movements Is Driving Change Around the World,

    https://time.com/collection/davos-2020/5764625/global-youth-movement/

3. The Hindu, Renata Dassallien, Responsible AI — the need for ethical guard rails, Mar 17, 2021

    https://www.thehindu.com/opinion/lead/responsible-ai-the-need-for-ethical-guard-rails/article34086236.ece